MW01245365

Living, Laughing, Loving Out Loud

Stories of the Heart

Helena Leet-Pellegrini

Copyright © 2021 Helena Leet-Pellegrini
All rights reserved.
Printed in the United States of America.

No part of this book may be used or reproduced in any manner whatsoever without the written permission of the author except in the case of brief quotations embodied in critical articles and reviews.

ISBN 978-1-7345189-5-5

Published by
Fringe Tree Press
Port Washington, New York

Cover and interior design by Maria Socolof.

For information and permissions, contact the publisher at www.fringetreepress.com.

Dedicated to

My mother and my daughter—

the two remarkable Marias in my life

Table of Contents

Preface

The stories contained in this book are derived from storytelling events performed in venues all across the country over the last fifteen years. I invite you to imagine them being told out loud, or even reading them out loud yourself. A Boston accent may accentuate the experience . . . make it even *betta*.

Lewis Carroll, author of *Adventures in Wonderland*, called stories "love gifts." These stories of the heart are my "love gifts" to you.

PART I

LIVING OUT LOUD

1

My Journey to Creative Expression

I don't know. It's hard to say when I really became aware of it—this impulse to create—the something deep inside that wants to express itself. Emile Zola said, "I came into the world to live out loud."

I think it was when I was little and began to go to the movies. Whenever the music came on, I imagined that the tiny space in front of my seat became an immense stage. And I would dance! I was eight years old when I took ballet lessons and learned to prance and twinkle through "Glow little glow worm, glow and glimmer . . . ." Everywhere I danced. It was wonderful. I was free. I came into the world to DANCE OUT LOUD!

Then . . . I don't know. Something happened. At a certain age, I realized I had a body and people might look at it. Self-consciousness set it, and those leotards that dancers wear became problematic.

No way, I thought. Bad enough when the family took you to the stupid beach, you had to put on a stupid bathing suit—*but to choose to put on something that was clingy and revealing?*

I once told a friend about my bathing suit problem. He said, "What are you worried about? There's nothing to you."

"Exactly," I said.

And then there was Dickie Harte, another dear friend. "Helena, don't worry," he said, "you're a perfect 36 . . . 12, 12, 12."

If dancing meant wearing leotards, then clearly I did not come into the world to DANCE OUT LOUD. What else could there be? I don't know.

Could I have come into the world to SING OUT LOUD? Not likely. I was one of those kids who learned to mouth the words, because my singing threw everybody off. I always knew the words of songs, but the tunes I heard in my head wouldn't come out of my mouth.

Not dancing. Not singing. What else? How about walking and talking? They had lessons for walking and talking way back when. They were called elocution lessons. And I took them! For the talking part you practiced enunciating—"'Twas brillig and the slithy toves did gyre and gimble in the wabe. All mimsy were the borogoves and the mome raths outgrabe."

For the walking and moving part, you practiced writing cursive letters in the air with your arms and legs. First a cursive capital *B* with your right hand. Then you add the mirror image with your left hand. Next you write a capital *B* with your right foot, and then with your left foot. Finally, hands and feet together—remembering to keep one foot planted—if you intend to remain standing.

When recital time came, I double-billed with my dear cousin, Eleanor, for a rendition of "Alice Blue Gown." Since she could really sing, she didn't get to walk and talk. She just stood there singing, while I sauntered in rhythm and gesticulated in rhyme: "In my sweet little Alice blue gown, / When I first wandered down into town, / . . . / 'Til it wilted I wore it, / I'll always adore it, / My sweet little Alice blue gown!" For my final flourish, using two hands and one leg, I decorated the air with a graceful and flowing . . . capital *G*.

Since I was showing some promise with this walking and talking, could it be that I came into the world to ACT OUT LOUD? *Let's try it!* I remember being on the stage one time, rehearsing.

I'm doing it . . . emoting and gesturing on stage. I'm feeling fine! That's when I heard the director somewhere out in the darkened audience say, "Don't use your hands so much. You don't look real."

"I don't look real? What are you telling me? I'm not real? You're saying I'm not real because of my hands. It's who I am. This is how I talk. I'm Italian and I took elocution lessons! What do you mean I'm not real?"

Now instead of throwing myself into the role I was supposed to be playing on stage, I was thrown into a personal existential crisis. *What does it really mean to be real? Am I real or am I an illusion? What if I'm not really here? Come to think of it, I've never seen my own face. I've seen the reflection of my face in the mirror. But I'm over here and the image is over there. So what's real? There or here. And if I'm not really here, then who's the one listening to these words coming of out my mouth?*

In short, there I was one moment trying to come out into the world to express myself, and in the next moment, I didn't even know if I had a self to express.

After that, the creative impulse went underground.

❧ ❧

Meanwhile, life goes on—get married, have three children in three years. It's a good life.

When the children began to go to school, the old yearnings came back. I'd have a little more time for myself. On one hand, I could keep the house cleaner. On the other hand, I could go back to school.

Keep the house cleaner? *I don't think so.*

Go back to school? *Okay . . . but in what?*

Maybe try theatre again? Maybe psychology, to get into the depths of psyche, learn more about self and other?

Theatre? . . . Psychology?

Graduate program in theatre at Brandeis with Morris Carnovsky? . . . Graduate program in psychology at Tufts?

During that time the big hit on Broadway was *O Calcutta*— actors getting naked on stage! *I don't think so! If that's the way theatre is going, then I'm not in it for sure.*

Again life goes on. Psychology's fulfilling. Family's fulfilling. Then life does that thing it can do. It delivers something that was never on your list of possibilities. You hear some doctor say, "You've got breast cancer."

By the way, I'm fine. That was over thirty years ago and even after a subsequently diagnosed bladder cancer, here I am. But that first cancer diagnosis came as a complete shock.

Psychosis I could have understood. Here's why. It was— *uh*—the sixties and I tried pot once. But I *really* didn't inhale, because I didn't know how. I never learned to smoke. When I tried to puff, I think the smoke got as far as the middle of my tongue. The next thing I knew, I was looking in the mirror and the whole left side of my face *left* the right side of my face. It took the whole night for my face to come back together again.

Psychosis—understandable. Cancer—out of the blue.

One minute you feel absolutely fine, and the next minute you could be dying. Moments like that definitely grab your attention. You are so totally engaged, absorbed, that suddenly you don't worry about the curtains you never put up on the windows. And your fear of flying? Gone. What fear of flying? I've got cancer.

Then something almost paradoxical happens. The awareness of dying can be very enlivening. Looking at death right in the face, the *feeling* is so *intense*—synapses are firing, shock waves of energy are coursing through your whole body. You realize—even in the depths of horror—how *alive* you are.

I remember the exact moment when the stirrings of life would no longer be denied. I was standing in the middle of my living room. There was quiet. I was quiet. I looked out our picture window. I saw the green lawn . . . the flowering bushes . . . the trees, leaves swaying and shimmering in the breeze, in the light . . . that white house up on the hill . . . the blue, cloudless sky.

Suddenly from nowhere . . . I heard myself humming . . . *hmm hmm hmm.* And then came the words from an old 1950s song, "I'm Gonna Live Till I Die."

Yes! I thought. *Until the very last, I AM gonna live. I'm gonna laugh, I'm gonna cry, I'm gonna dance, I'm gonna fly.*

Cancer clearly brings home the truth that all we really have is moment after moment of *now* aliveness. At that point, the old stirrings were revived. And with that the call to live out loud became a shout. "If not now, WHEN?" I remembered

Marisa Tomei in the movie *My Cousin Vinny* saying, as she kept stomping her foot, "The clock is ticking!"

But once again. What's *my* form of living out loud? How about SOLO PERFORMANCE? I actually took a workshop on solo performing. When it was my turn, I stood up on stage. I couldn't move. Nothing came out. There I was up in front of the class—paralyzed. Finally, the teacher said, "What's going on?"

"I don't want to draw attention to myself."

"Wait a minute. Let me get this straight. You signed up for a course in solo performing and you don't want to draw attention to yourself?"

"Yeah," I whispered, "is that going to be a problem?"

How about SINGING? Maybe something's changed. A few lessons?

I went to a voice teacher who'd performed in a Bulgarian women's chorus. I would practice the vocal warm up, remembering to breathe—over and over again—br-e-a-th-e. I "sang" unintelligible syllables I imagined were Bulgarian. *Senza ni-naaaa—senza ni-naaaa.* My musician son told me I sounded like a gaggle of geese in distress. Forget singing.

How about COMEDY? Someone once suggested I do stand-up comedy, so I took a mini course from Dick Doherty, known as the Godfather of Boston Comedy. At some point, everyone in the class had to stand up and tell one joke. This is the joke I had prepared in advance:

"I just had a birthday. I told a friend I was fifty-five years old. He said, 'That's not an age. It's a speed limit.'"

Unexpectedly, Dick Doherty responded, "Some kind of friend that was."

"Yeah," and then, unrehearsed, I added, "and another dear friend sent me a birthday card that read, 'See this egg in my left hand? See this frying pan in my right hand? This is the effect of the aging process on your brain.'" I slammed the invisible frying pan in my right hand onto the invisible egg in my left hand, grimacing in disgust as my fingers mimicked the gooey, sticky, raw egg travelling down my arm.

Dick Doherty said, "If you want to, you could do stand up."

I didn't speak. With my mouth agape, and my face registering horror, I thought: *No way!*

Dick Doherty followed up with, "You don't want to hear that, do you?"

Of course I didn't want to hear that. If I did stand up, then I'd have to go to comedy clubs. I can't smoke; you know that. I'd just cough and choke. I don't really drink. I have a shunt from my mouth to my brain. One teaspoon of wine and call me Loopy. And anyway, those comedy clubs stay open till all hours. At this age, I go to bed early. Why was he telling me I could do stand up?

How about ACTING again? Maybe this time *classical* theatre would be my thing. I've never seen a Shakespearian production performed in the nude.

For my acting class, I practiced words spoken by Lady Macbeth in the scene where she fiercely berates Macbeth, attempting to reignite his waning courage to follow through with the murder of Duncan, the king he longs to replace.

"Fie, my lord" . . . I bellow as regally as I can, reminding myself to stand tall, majestic.

"A soldier, and afeard?" . . . I forcefully raise my right arm and point an admonishing index finger at a wilting, would-be monarch.

"Was the hope drunk / Wherein you dressed yourself?" . . . I lose focus and start to slump. I imagine a puppeteer pulls up on the invisible strings attached to the top of my head, and says, "Helena, you're supposed to be a queen."

"Hath it slept since?" . . . I don't use my hands too much. I want to look "real." When I gesticulate with one hand, I make sure the other lies dormant at my side.

"And wakes it now to look so green and pale / At what it did so freely?" Over and over again I practiced. My British accent improved. When a London native asked, "Where did you learn to master that accent?" I felt I was finally getting somewhere. The problem came when I practiced in front of a mirror.

Oh no! Look at me. I'm too ethnic. Too Italian-looking. And however high the puppeteer pulls up on my invisible strings, I'm still short.

Who'd ever cast me as British royalty?

How about PERFORMANCE ART? I didn't even know what that was, but I liked the sound of it. So I looked up the definition on the internet. "Performance Art: that wild and crazy hybrid of theater, sculpture, stand-up comedy, private ritual and public rant." *Is that what I'm going to do?*

I searched further on the internet and read a description of a "fascinating and accomplished Australian performance artist who puts her nude body into dramatic relationship with the Earth."

Then it showed a picture of a vast Australian desert landscape with a dead tree towering in the foreground. There she was against this barren expanse, hanging from the tree, noose around her neck, naked. What am I supposed to do where I live? How do I put my body in dramatic relationship to the Earth? How's this for a marquee: *Performance artist, Helena Leet-Pellegrini, appearing nightly as road kill along the Massachusetts Turnpike—no clothes.*

෴

Still yearning to express myself, still filled with doubts, confusion, ambivalence, fear, paralysis, and self-consciousness, I wondered, *How do we get to be the way we are? What forges us?* Well, you know what "they" say. "They" say it has something to do with the families we come from. *Maybe our parents?*

One thing we know is that we've all got *stuff.* Yours could be different from mine, but we all have it. I figure that we get two kinds of stuff from each parent.

You could say . . . the upside and the downside.

The stuff that works and the stuff we end up working on for the rest of our lives.

As Edna St. Vincent Millay said, "It's not true that life is one damn thing after another; it's one damn thing over and over."

෴

What did I get from my father?

On the upside . . . the gift. Unconditional love. Not bad. You just knew. And then there was his sense of fun, joy, and the way he laughed from the bottom of his toes all the way up to the top of his head.

He was a terribly ineffective disciplinarian. I remember one time when I was little, just standing there, waiting to be scolded. I wasn't sure exactly what I'd done, but I sensed a reprimand coming. Dad walked right up to me. Suddenly, he burst out laughing, turned around, ran into another room, and closed the door, as if I wouldn't be able to hear him. "Mae," he calls out to my mother, "she's so cute!"

My Italian dad would seriously tell people he just met that he could speak French. Then he would fearlessly launch into badly accented babble: "*Bonjour! Vive la piscine de la tour, de l'amour. En garde. Voilà! Au revoir.*"

Some people giggled, some didn't.

When he told a story, between his Italian accent and irrepressible laughter, no one understood a word he said, but they'd laugh anyway from pure contagion and delight.

On the downside . . . let's say cognitive consistency was a challenge. Here's a life lesson from my father:

I was young, in school. One day a new kid, Lois, came to my class and sat behind me. I turned around to get acquainted with her, lifting my arm to lean on the back of my chair. As we talked, she mentioned she was black. I looked at my arm. I looked at her arm. She's lighter than I am. I didn't get it.

I went to my father, "Dad, how come I'm dark, but I'm white, and she's light, but she's black?"

"I'll tell you how it is . . . black is black and white is white and black is white and white is black. Now you know."

Hello? Where is this man? He sits there—in perfect calm—while I try to imagine: In what universe is this a viable statement? At the very least you're thrown into a puzzlement. Nothing's simple.

Here's another life lesson. We're discussing family feuds and what you can do to make peace. This, he says in one paragraph: "Blood is the thing. It's blood that counts. It's up to the blood relatives to make any moves. I'm only the in-law, so it's not up to me to make the peace. Unless I go over there first and make the peace because blood doesn't count."

What am I supposed to get outta that?

He had a way of speaking in opposites. When I was learning to drive, he took me out for practice—once. It was the early fifties, way before automatic transmissions. You have to contend with a stick shift on the floor, your hands on the wheel, a clutch and a gas pedal that go up and down. Both hands and feet are moving, and then you have to stick your hand out the window to turn left, and circle your wrist to turn right. It's not easy. It's hard to keep track of everything at once.

We were on Lake Avenue, a big broad street in Worcester, Massachusetts. No sidewalks, hardly any traffic. I'm driving straight ahead when I hear, "More to the right. More to the right. More to the right. . . . Okay, now up the lawn."

I'm actually headed for somebody's lawn! That's when I figure out "more to the right" doesn't mean more to the right.

I'm driving around a corner. My father says, "What are you doing? Why don't you go faster?"

I obey.

Next corner he says. "Okay, go ahead, faster, more gas."

I obey.

At the third corner he says, "That's it, more gas, faster. Okay now, *two* wheels!"

That's when I realize faster doesn't mean faster.

"What's the matter with you?" he says. "What are you listening to me for? Just because I said it? You gotta see for yourself. You're going too fast. You're going to hit the parked car!"

So I had to remember doing all these new car maneuvers, and on top of that, flip everything into its opposite. Right is left. Fast is slow. *What?* Because he talked so inside out, upside down and backward, in our Italian dialect, we said he talked "*come un giornale strazzata*"—like a ripped up newspaper.

As I grew up, this man couldn't understand why I kept saying, "I don't know. . . . It could be. . . . Maybe it's . . . I don't know."

When I came back from college, I was still saying pretty much the same thing. He said, "Again, you don't know? Four years in college, you come back and you're still saying, 'I don't know. I don't know!'"

"Dad, after four years of college I have more questions, and I know less now than I did before."

"*Mah*, how can you know less than nothing?"

"I don't know, Dad, but now that you say it, I'm thinking that 'less than nothing' is an interesting idea. I think I have to keep going to school to find out more and more about 'less than nothing,' or even less and less about 'less than nothing.'" *What am I saying?*

What did I get from my mother?

On the upside . . . there are the gifts: the love and the caring. She was the steady, constant nurturer. You always knew you came first.

When it came to food—the primary source of nurturance in Italian families—my mother made sure that everyone's tastes were accommodated before her own. This meant that she sometimes prepared three meals for four people . . . one for me, one for my brother, and one for her husband (and herself).

One day when I was in third grade and taking ballet lessons, my mother called Miss Kerrigan, the school principal, to request my dismissal a few minutes early that afternoon. I was to go to a special pre-recital rehearsal and have a costume fitting for my sparkling gold lamé tutu. Miss Kerrigan let my mother know in no uncertain terms that she would not dismiss me, that the reason was insufficient and that school policy would not allow it.

A generally gentle and demur woman, my mother became bold and assertive on my behalf. She went over Miss Kerrigan's head, called the School Department, and learned that as a parent she had every right to have her request for dismissal honored. I was dismissed, and my little glow worm in lamé glimmered extra bright that day, because my mother was there for me. I always wondered why after that incident, Miss Kerrigan, who'd always called me Helena, began calling me Henrietta. But it's my mother I hold in memory, she who would go beyond her comfort zone for her eight-year-old-maybe-could-be-would-be ballerina daughter. In this regard, she was known in the family by the nickname: the steel marshmallow.

On the downside . . . my mother, like pretty much all the other women in our family, worshipped at the temple of fear.

To give you a flavor: You're a kid, you're at home, and you've climbed halfway up the stairs. Your mother comes around the corner. She screams, *"ARHGH!"* shoving her hand into her mouth, chomping down on her index finger ready to draw blood.

"What is it, Mom!"

"You're halfway up the stairs!"

"I know."

"If you go up, you'll trip. If you come down, you'll fall."

"Thanks, Mom. Now I can't move."

Then there are bikes. I come from a big extended Italian family, eleven grandchildren. None of us had a bicycle. I remember as an adult being truly shocked when an acquaintance asked, very earnestly, "Why couldn't you have bicycles?"

"Why? What do you mean . . . why? Bikes go on the street. Streets have cars and trucks. You die. That's why."

Doesn't everybody know this?

As you get older, this loving, giving family says: "Go be free, do anything you want. The world is yours. Go! . . . Just one thing. You can't cross the street." Do you know how long it takes to go around the world in my old neighborhood— without crossing the street? Tops, five minutes. When you come back home, your obviously agitated mother at the door asks, "Where were you?"

"I went around the world, and I didn't cross the street."

Smiling with relief she says, "Oh, that's good . . . and what did you see?"

"I saw the side of the house, the back of the house, the other side of the house, and you at the front door."

"That's nice. I'm so happy for you!"

"Ma. I'm twenty-eight years old."

◈◈

I come by my terror honestly. I was trained by this exquisitely Baroque—no, no, Rococo—worrier. Everything is dangerous.

Streets, heights, water. Every place is dangerous. If you're outside the house, they're going to attack you. If you're inside the house, they're going to break in . . . and they're going to attack you.

There might be two slightly safe things you can do. One is eating, because we're Italian; the other is resting in bed. My mother would often say, "Why don't you go lie down and rest, honey? You shouldn't do too much." This after I have no idea what I've done all day. I think the principle here is that not moving is good, because things are more likely to happen when there is motion. If I don't move, I'll be okay. Of course, on the flip side, if I'm not moving, I could already be dead. *See!* There's always the next thing we have to worry about!

And I kept learning about the stuff I got from my mom. One day I went to visit her when she was at St Patricks Manor Nursing Home. She wasn't in her room. Staff directed me to the Tara Lounge, where residents assemble for special events. As I approached the Lounge, I heard a live band playing music from *West Side Story*. There was my Mom lined up in the second of five rows of wheelchairs and walkers. After greeting her with a nod, I went as unobtrusively as possible to find an empty seat off to the side. It was so great to see how music brightened those ever-aging eyes.

At one point the singer started a lively Polish polka. All the social activity volunteers began to dance, clap their hands, and move around the room working to engage the residents. It was irresistible. Of course, I got up, too. This was a chance for me to let the joy of music and life flow through me. It was a moment of aliveness . . . the aliveness that we know will necessarily die, but as it fades, why should life be devoid of precious moments like this?

In that spirit, I hand-danced with my mother, and with some of the others. I clapped as I polkaed up and down the aisles. When it was over I asked, "How was that, Mom? Did you enjoy the music? What did you think?"

She talked about the woman next to her who had snickered at the event, at all these people making fools of themselves.

"But what did *you* think, Mom?"

"Well, people were watching you and smiling at you."

"Yeah?"

"Well, your children and your husband weren't there, so you did it. But don't do it in front of them."

"Why?"

"They would be embarrassed. That's how they are."

"Were you embarrassed?"

"Yes."

"Why?"

"Because the people will think you're a bum. I know you're not. I know you grew up nice and decent. But they'll think you're a bum. They'll think you do . . . that," she says as she raises her eyebrows, widens her eyes, and thrusts her head up and away. "And . . . *that*," she says as she raises her eyebrows, widens her eyes, and thrusts her head up, *up*, and away.

I do . . . that . . . and that? *Aah*, now I understand. In her vernacular, "bum" means *putana*, whore.

No wonder I get self-conscious! I'm afraid that the minute I get up and speak or move and people are looking at me (God forbid they're smiling), I know what's going to happen. In the next second, they're all going to stand up and shout, "BUM, BUM. You're a *putana*, BUM!"

∽ ೕ

Here I am, ever wanting to live out loud, continuing to work on the downside stuff—the confusion, the speaking in opposites from my father, the fear from my mother. But now I imagine that even to the downside of stuff, there's an upside.

As for confusion, it keeps you curious, keeps the mind flexible. There's something expansive about turning things around, looking at them in different ways. Heads is the opposite of tails, but when we take the larger view, we see they're both on the same coin. If we're talking about, say, skin color, black and white are opposites, but they're both on the same coin—called human beings. From that larger view, "black is black, white is white, and black is white and white is black" makes sense—one humanity.

And then there's this wondrous thing called clarity. Everybody loves clarity—the clouds part, the sun shines, the birds sing. But why shouldn't we love confusion just as much—with all its murky muddleness? Think about it. In order to get clear about something, what were we the moment before? . . . *Aah* . . . confused! Confusion—a gateway to clarity. Both necessary steps in the one dance of being alive and learning.

And what did Salvador Dalí say? "You have to systematically create confusion, it sets creativity free. Everything that is contradictory creates life." That man could have known my father. They both had mustaches.

As for fear, one thing I do know. It puts you on high alert. There's a lot of energy bottled up in that fear. If I don't think about *what* I'm afraid of, but focus on the energy inside the fear, I realize it's an intense, powerful energy. And when I dive into that fierce energy and use it to come out in the world, in that moment I know I'm alive.

And then there's this wondrous thing called courage. Everybody loves courage. How could there even be such a thing as courage, if first you didn't have . . . danger, risk, fear? I can use the energy of fear to fuel my courage. Courage—*coraggio*, from the word heart—*cuore*. Time to express myself with courage . . . with all my heart.

Okay, Mom. I'm gonna do it.

I'm on stage now, Mom, and it's not the imaginary stage in an eight-year-old mind.

My heart is pounding.

There's a trembling inside my body.

It's the energy! I feel it. And it's moving me!

I'm ready, Mom.

I'm gonna practice living out loud, being alive.

Even if they look at me, Mom, smiling or not smiling,

I'm gonna sing . . . right now.

And I sing. And Edith Piaf is there. And it's "*La Vie en Rose.*" And it's in French. And then it's in English. And I'm *not* wondering if the tune I hear in my head is coming out of my mouth. I'm simply lost in song. And it lasts a forever-moment. And when it's over, the entire audience stands. And together we repeat the final refrain—*La Vie en Rose.*

Thank you, Mom.

Thank you, Dad.

Thanks for the STUFF.

ALL of it.

I love you.

❧ Epilogue: How I Found Storytelling ❧

It happened about eighteen years ago.

At that time, my daughter, Maria, her husband, and their two adorable little girls had been living in the apartment attached to our house. One day she announced that the family was moving to Maryland. My heart sank. My first thought was, "How could my son-in-law do this to *me* . . . take away my three girls?" When my sanity was restored, I realized they were not my girls, and it was time to turn my attention inward, to do my own thing, to create.

I found a venue called *Out Spoken Word* in Natick, Massachusetts, hosted by storyteller, Libby Franck, and steeled myself to sign up for an open mic slot. Michaela, my eight-year-old granddaughter, whose family hadn't moved out yet, became my attentive listener as I practiced a five-minute story. She was my first coach. Michaela gave a couple of little smiles, and at the end, said, "That's good, but next time a few less *ums* and *ers*."

When Libby invited me to be a featured teller at *Out Spoken Word*, I said yes, but only after I checked to see that indeed she was talking to me. "Living Out Loud: My Journey to Creative Expression" was the first feature-length story I ever told, and now is the first chapter of my book.

After that I found Tuesday nights at Story Space in Cambridge with the pied piper of storytelling—Brother Blue, a.k.a. Dr. Hugh Morgan Hill, a lanky black man. There he was, dressed in all shades of blue and bedecked with blue butterflies.

I flashed back to a moment that had grabbed my attention a couple years earlier. I was at The Butterfly Place in Westford, Massachusetts with Michaela. All manner of colorful butterflies everywhere. Dazzling. At one moment a beautiful, vibrant blue butterfly came to rest just above my heart. And there it stayed. While other butterflies kept fluttering around, this one just stayed and stayed. After a while, I asked a stranger to take a picture, so I could capture on film what had so captured me.

And now here before me was a blue, butterfly man, who, with his beloved wife Ruth, welcomed everyone to Story Space, where every story was considered a gift for our shared humanity. Blue believed that storytelling could change the world. Of his own telling, he would say, "I tell stories from the middle of the middle of me to the middle of the middle of you."

Aah, for sure, storytelling clearly became an answer to the question I had been asking, "What's *my* form of creative expression?" It works for me in many ways.

I don't feel constricted by storytelling. There's no place in which it has to happen, like a theatre or comedy club. Stories can be told anywhere. Nobody asks me to take my clothes off or even put on a bathing suit, and if I want to, I can arrange to be in bed early—say, no later than 9:30 at night.

I'm enlivened by storytelling. I get to share with others not only the *HA-HA*'s of life, but the *AHA*'s of life—moments when we wake up to new awarenesses. And then sometimes, the *AAAH*'s of life, when the soul finds a place to rest.

And I am in *awe* of the magical and healing power of stories to connect us all. When we share our stories, we get to see that whatever our unique paths, whatever our individual twists and turns in life, we all belong to that singular, extraordinary story I call *Human Beings Being Human.*

2

The Luigi Code

It began with a reverie. I found myself pondering the mysteries of life. Some have asked: "What's it all about, Alfie?" or "Is that all there is, my friends?" My question was: *What's it like to be free?* Whenever I would meet someone named Freeman, I'd get heart palpitations. *Free . . . man. What's that?*

I grew up in a sheltered Italian family in Worcester, Massachusetts. And what I got from them, might be called . . . mixed messages.

On one hand it was: "Go. Be free. The world is yours, honey. Whatever you want." On the other hand it was: "*Ooh, ooh, ooh,* be careful."

If you go in the water, you're going to drown in the waves; if you climb up that hill, you're going to plunge to your death; if you go by yourself to the drinking fountain, you're going to get kidnapped and murdered; if you look a man in the eye, you're going to be raped! *Get the picture?*

Now you know my family. As you might guess, I didn't develop into a very adventurous person. But at a time of reflection, when I wanted to break free, live out loud, I decided to play a little game with myself. "Okay, Helena, pretend. Imagine you *are* really free. The whole world is yours. Go! Do! Anywhere, anything! No one has to know but you!" I closed my eyes and took a deep breath. Slowly . . . words bubbled up into my consciousness . . . I heard . . . St. Louis, Missouri. *St. Louis Missouri?* Of all the places on this glorious planet, I get St. Louis, Missouri? I love the ocean. Missouri is some landlocked place. The only thing I know about St. Louis is that it has a golden arch. . . . Another image bubbles up, and I see myself running through the Gateway Arch in St. Louis. I'm looking for more freedom in my life, and the best I can do . . . is run through half a McDonald's sign?

After a while a little light bulb goes off. My grandfather's name is Luigi DeSantis. In Italian, that's Louis of the Saints . . . St. Louis!

What I believe is that stories are alive and they call us to them. "Is that you, Papa Luigi? Is there something I'm supposed to look at, something to unravel here? What's the story?"

I've always felt some ambivalence, some reticence about telling Papa Luigi stories. When I think of Papa, I often remember an old photograph taken in 1913 that always intrigued me. He's wearing a big, black, flouncy tie and standing with a group of men, women, and children at what looks like a Sunday gathering in East Park, Worcester. I was young when I found the picture and asked my mother about it.

She said, "The family doesn't talk about this very much, but these are anarchists. Papa Luigi was one of them. See this man?" she said pointing to one of the figures. "His name was Bartolomeo Vanzetti. When he was in Worcester, he stayed in Nana and Papa Luigi's house. A few years later he and another anarchist, Nicola Sacco . . . well, they were arrested for robbery and murder. But a lot of people believed they were innocent, and that they were really arrested for their beliefs and for being immigrants. People from all over the world, some important people, tried to save them. But in the end, Sacco and Vanzetti were executed."

I was about eight. I *heard* the words.

⟜⟜

A couple of years ago, I was telling some people I'd just met about this 1913 picture of my grandfather with Vanzetti. Turns out I was speaking to a historian whose specific focus is the Sacco and Vanzetti case. He told me he was currently looking into the year that Vanzetti spent in Worcester—the year that Vanzetti might well have been radicalized as an anarchist—1913.

What are the chances?

"Is that you again, Papa Luigi?"

The historian got very excited, he said: "It's your moral imperative to find that picture."

"Okay, Papa!" The call is getting louder. Now I feel I *have* to tell the stories.

At that point my mother was ninety-six and living at St Patricks nursing home. I became exquisitely aware that there might not be much time left to ask her more about the old days. Up until she was ninety, my mother's memory was pretty intact, but the years after that took their toll. People and times and events would cascade into one another.

But on one particular day, when I wanted to eke out whatever I still could, her memory was amazing! She was clear and back to being a little girl sitting at her father's knee.

"I loved his ideas—my sisters and my brother always wanted to go out and play, but I loved being in the little room with him where he would read Dante and Zola, listen to Verdi, and tell me all about them. But when I grew older, I saw how different he was. I got upset. I wanted him to be like all the other fathers, who went to church."

She saw me taking notes.

"What are you doing? Are you writing this down? Are you going to tell this to anyone? Who are you going to tell?"

At ninety-six, when dementia was wreaking havoc with her memory, when she may or may not remember her own husband and children, the fear was still palpable. She let me know this was a story not to be told *out loud*.

That day at St Patricks, I said, "Don't be afraid, Mom, it's okay now to tell the story. That was a long time ago."

She looked at me: "It's okay now? Really?"

She got me with that question, because my next thought was: *I don't know if it's really okay—even today! So now what? To tell or not to tell.*

❧ What I Remember ❧

My memories of Papa Luigi are scattered.

I remember how Papa looked. A trim, elegant man. Not elegant measured by the clothes he wore, but by his presence. Papa had a full mustache, beneath dark, lively, twinkling eyes. Black wavy hair that hardly grayed through his seventies, eighties, and even nineties. Papa died at ninety-nine, three months short of his 100th birthday.

I remember a *gentle*-man. Papa loved to fish. But without bait or a hook. He didn't want to hurt the fish. "The beau-ty of fishing," he would say, "is not in-a catching the fish." And there was that time in Florida when Papa got mugged. He was about ninety years old when some punks knocked him to the ground to steal his wallet. Maybe he had five dollars. "Why they knock-a me down?" said Papa. "If somebody ask-a me for money, they need it more than me. If they ask-a me, I give it to them. Why they gotta knock-a me down?"

I remember growing up in the family compound in Worcester where three-decker houses sprouted up everywhere at the turn of the last century. In our three-decker, Nana and Papa Luigi lived on the first floor. My Auntie Jo lived on the second floor. We lived on the third floor, and my uncle Libro lived next to the three-decker in what we all called "the little house." Auntie Bina moved into the second floor of her mother-in-law's house across the street. And everyone cried when Auntie Artie moved away—one mile down the road.

I remember that everyone was in such a hurry for the family to assimilate, to become American as soon as possible. The chant was "Don't speak Italian to the kids." Only Papa resisted. Italian was *la lingua più bella del mondo*—the most beautiful language in the world. He didn't want to *rovinare la bocca* . . . ruin his mouth.

Parlare italiano è come si canta . . . Speaking Italian is like singing. The family was actually happy that Papa hardly spoke English. "That way *they* won't be able to understand all those things he's saying." *What things? Who's THEY?*

Papa liked everything to be simple, uncomplicated. His food—fresh and healthy. No thick Sunday gravies, as we called them—the tomato sauce that cooked for hours, with braccioles, meatballs, and sometimes pork to give it yet a deeper, richer flavor. No. Papa loved quick marinara sauces with fresh tomatoes that jumped from his garden into the pan and onto the plate.

I remember watching intently as Papa prepared a favorite dish of his: *arance sotto l'acqua* . . . literally, oranges under water. I remember thinking, as a kid, *what bland and boring foods Papa likes.* Yet, I was transported whenever I watched him peel an orange impeccably with his knife, slowly slice the orange into rounds, lay them on a plate and then drizzle them with water and olive oil. What else he sprinkled on I can't remember. Then he would eat. But he wasn't *just* eating. There was something more.

Fifty years later, I was in a restaurant somewhere in *Sicilia*, and we were served blood oranges covered in exquisitely flavored water. With my first bite, the taste sensation was so startling that I had an epiphany—*Oh Papa, now I get it. There's a difference between the name of something and the essence of that thing itself. Orange . . . the word, and O-R-A-N-G-E, the experience . . . when senses come alive.*

I remember Papa's little room, the same room where my mother sat listening to his teachings. This was the place that held the seeds of what made Papa different. There were stacks of Italian newspapers, books in Italian—among them his treasured volume of Dante Alighieri's (and I still almost catch Papa's voice as he would proclaim): *La Divina Commedia.*

On Saturday afternoons, the opera was broadcast live from the Met into Papa's little room. *La Traviata* was his favorite opera and he loved to quote Giuseppe Verdi, who pronounced that the three most important things in life were: *il pane, l'amore, e la musica*—bread, love, and music. Sometimes you could hear scratchy records playing on the old Victrola.

"Who's that, Papa?" I'd ask.

Papa would sing out delightedly, caressing every syllable, "Enrico Caruso."

The cellar was where Papa engaged in his cabinetmaking craft, and because he was an artisan, he was known as Master Luigi. I remember the big saws, all kinds of carpentry tools, stacks of wood that he made into bookcases, chests, and chairs for his children and grandchildren. And, of course, there were the endless jars of canned tomatoes that made sure we would capture that sunny summery taste all winter long.

I remember Papa coveted very little. He loved his cigars—Panatelas, Coronas—the cheaper the better. You couldn't buy Papa any gift more satisfying than those old stogies.

We'd try: "Papa, here's a new sweater."

"*Eeh*, I'm-a got a sweater."

Papa had all old clothes, but clean—my grandmother Marianina took care of that!

People would say, "Master Luigi, why donna you get-a some new clothes? You wear same-a thing all-a time. You could-a look better."

Now, our Italian community in Worcester was fairly contained at the time.

So Papa replied, "It's me, Luigi. *Mah*, why I gotta change? Why? I gotta make a show? Everybody here knows-a me."

One day, a group of people from our community went to visit the big city, Bos'ton. They were strolling along

Washington Street, when who do they see walking toward them? None other than Papa, wearing the same old clothes. "Master Luigi, *mah*, you in-a Bos'ton now. What are you doin' dress-a like dat?" "It's me, Luigi. *Mah*, why I gotta change? Why? I gotta make a show? Nobody here knows-a me."

ᴖ *Stories, History, and Philosophy* ᴖ

Some of these stories about Papa Luigi I remember, and some are what my mother told me. One time she said, "When you were young, you used to want me to tell the family stories. I would tell them, but I would always change them a little to make them nice."

[Wait a minute. Stop. Time for an aside: What do we really know about all the stories we hear? Memories are not facts. I have my memories. My mother has hers. Then I learn she's added to the stories—made them "nice" for me. On top of that, I'm hearing the same stories at different ages, filtering them through my eight-year-old, twelve-year-old, twenty-five-year-old, forty-year-old, sixty-year-old mind. On top of that she's telling those same stories at different ages and sensibilities in her life. . . . So really, what is the story here?]

Papa Luigi was born in *Bisceglie, Provincia di Bari* in Italy in 1879, the first-born son of Maria and Pasquale DeSantis. His two younger brothers were Emmanuele and Armando. They all agreed their father Pasquale, an educated man, a customs official, was a beau-ti-ful father. "He bought us things, brought us places, spent time with us."

Papa Luigi was nineteen years old in 1898 when he went into the Italian navy—reluctantly, we were told—and came back filled with anarchist ideas that had been sweeping Italy in the last half of the 1800s.

[Another aside: What I've come to learn about anarchism is that it is not, as often thought, all about chaos and disorganization, every man for himself. Howard Zinn discusses that the beliefs central to anarchism are:

(1) Social organization and cooperation are natural;
(2) People are fundamentally good but can be corrupted by the very institutions they create;
(3) Individual freedom is essential; and
(4) Any authority, individual, state, church, or corporation that seeks to dominate and exploit is rejected.

He wrote: "Anarchism believes that if we can create an egalitarian society without extremes of poverty and wealth, and join hands across all national boundaries to cooperate in work and play, we will not need police forces, prisons, armies, or war, because the underlying causes of these will be gone."]

This was the kind of philosophy that Papa was developing throughout his twenties back in Italy. Papa would say: "*Per il potere, ammazzano l'umanità.*" For power, they will destroy humanity.

৵ ৵

In 1908, when Papa Luigi was twenty-nine, he married twenty-two-year-old Marianina Lorrusso, my grandmother. He was so poor he didn't have one single *lira* in his pocket. Marianina had to pay for the honeymoon hotel. She had run away with Luigi, eloped, because her family was eyeing her for some other man and she would have none of that.

Now this is one story that got shifted as I got older. It seems that Nana and Papa really didn't get married when they eloped. Papa didn't believe in the *institution* of marriage, because the wife has to promise to obey the husband.

"What? He owns her? That's-a no freedom. You don't own anybody." But the social stigma of "living in sin" was too much for Marianina and she wanted to marry. Papa became caught in the creative tension between what was ideal and what was going to be practical given the prevailing social mores. Papa relented and after two months he went to get a marriage license. But, as the story continued, he was adamant that he would not go into the church to be married. Neighbors finally convinced Papa to get a priest, but the priest had to come to the house. It's been said that the priest whispered to Papa, "I believe like you, but—let's please Marianina."

Papa Luigi never wanted to admit he'd been married by a priest. For him it was always, "Church-a no good. *Cristo* (Christ) good. Church. No."

When I was young (about eight and ready to receive first communion), I asked my mother: "Why doesn't Papa like the priests and the church?"

She said, "He doesn't believe they tell the people the truth. He believes that the priests, like the politicians, will lie to keep the people ignorant, so they can have more control over them. But when I grew up," she continued, "I got curious and checked out different churches for myself. I'd come back and tell my father the churches seemed just fine. We would argue.

But he never stopped us from believing whatever we wanted to."

And a generation later, we grandchildren, for kicks, sometimes would dare to taunt Papa. We could get a little fire going. All we had to do was mention church. "Papa," we'd chant, "church is good."

"Church-a, no good."

"Papa when you pass the church you bow your head, like this," we'd say dropping our chins to our chests.

"No! . . . I go-a like this," declared Papa, as he thrust his chin upward and outward.

Truth be known, Nana Marianina was also, let's say, not enamored of the church. It seems, as the story goes, that when she was about thirteen, a priest invited her to go with him someplace behind the altar. I was never told what happened, but that was the last time Marianina herself went to church. Getting married was all about holding social standing in the community.

❧ *Naming* ❧

Soon after Papa Luigi and Nana Marianina were married, they came to this country. It was 1909. My mother, Maria, conceived in Italy, was born in the US in 1910, to be followed by three sisters and a brother.

There is a clear pattern to naming children in Italian families. First-born son is named after paternal grandfather, second-born son after maternal grandfather, first-born daughter after paternal grandmother, second-born daughter after maternal grandmother. After you run out of parents on both sides, you start naming children after uncles and aunts in descending order of their birth.

The reader doesn't need to get any of this. This is only interesting if you've ever wondered why in Italian families so many first cousins have the same name—a bunch of Domenics or Anthonys for the boys, a bunch Marias or Angelinas for the girls.

At first Papa kept to this pattern for naming his children. His first daughter, my mother, was given Luigi's mother's name, Maria. A year later in 1911, second daughter was given Marianina's mother's name, Giuseppina (this is Josephine, my Auntie Jo). But the third daughter, born in 1913, was given a name more reflective of Papa's stance in life. Everything natural is a wonder—never to be taken for granted. *Che bella cosa* (what a beautiful thing) *na jurnata 'e sole* (the sun rose). A surprising miracle everyday! So third daughter becomes Alba—translation Dawn—and in the diminutive, Albina, my Auntie Bina.

By the time the fourth daughter arrived in 1916, Papa went further out on the limb. We always called her Auntie Artie, for short, because her name was Artea (A-R-T-E-A). Or so we thought. What we eventually learned was that Papa's name for her had no *r* in it. It was Atea (A-T-E-A) (translation atheist). The family had to do something with *that* name to make it *not* be what it was. So they slipped in that little *r* and wrote A-R-T-E-A. Maybe people would think the name had something to do with "art" or "artist."

Funny thing is, when the family speaks her name, there's no difference. See, we're from Massachusetts and we don't pronounce *r*'s that come after the letter *a*. You know, "Pahk the cah in the Havahd Yahd." So before her name was changed, we called her Auntie *Ahti*. Now that her name was "nice," we called her—Auntie *Ahti*.

Happily, Luigi and Marianina's fifth child was the long-awaited son, my Uncle Libro, born in 1919. We always laughed as kids because Uncle Libro translates as Uncle Book. Or so we thought. But this is the story we heard later:

When my uncle was born, Papa Luigi proudly wrote to his father in Italy: "Now I have a son and I have given him your name—Pasquale DeSantis."

Pasquale DeSantis wrote back, "Why give him such an old-fashioned name? This is a new time. Give him a new name."

So Papa dashed off to City Hall, unbeknownst to his wife, to change the baby's name. When he returned, he announced to Marianina: "The baby's new name is 'Libero Sono.'" Translation: I am free.

But times were tough in 1919. You couldn't really show your true stripes. Once again to accommodate the outside world, one little letter gets changed. But this time, instead of adding a letter, we drop one out. Taking the *e* out of Libero, gives you Libro. Now instead of Uncle "I Am Free," we have a much more acceptable Uncle "Book."

Papa and his fellow compatriots were of a similar inclination when it came to naming their children. There was another boy in that community named Libero. And two of my mother's closest friends were named Ora (Now) and Edea (Idea).

I can imagine what it was like when those families got together for Sunday Socials and they had to gather the children around for the most important event of the day . . . eating. I can hear it now. "Let's go kids," as the mothers shout and wave their arms, "time-a to eat. Get ovah here! *Eh* . . . Dawn, Now,

Idea, Atheist, I Am Free, the other I Am Free. Get ovah here. Now!"

❧ *Work* ❧

The years from 1910 to 1920 were difficult for immigrant families. The children were growing up, and it was harder and harder to make ends meet. There's always been a question in the family about Papa and his relationship to work. He'd have a job here, work a few days there—nothing consistent or reliable. What's the story?

There were remarks made in the family like:

➢ "Well, you know, Papa never busted his hump."
➢ "He was always futzing around the cellar making picture frames."
➢ "Nana used to yell at him to get up off the couch, and he'd answer, 'Leave-a me alone. Go way! I gotta nails in-a my head.'"

What we do know is that Papa loved to converse intently with like-minded friends . . . sit in his rocking chair . . . read a book . . . listen to an opera . . . smoke his old stogie down to the nubbins.

People would say, "Master Luigi, you do-a nice woodwork. You could-a work a little bit more, sell-a something, and make-a some money."

"And *then* what I'm-a gonna do?"

"Well, you could bring in-a some other people, work-a with you, work-a *for* you. You start-a da business. Make-a *more* money."

"And *then* what I'm-a gonna do?"

"Then you keep-a growing da business, it gets *so* big . . . you *really* make-a more money."

"And *then* what I'm-a gonna do?"

"Then one-a day, when you make enuf-a money, you sell-a da business, and then you can take it easy . . . do *whatever* you want to do!"

"Let-a me think-a here . . . You telling-a me . . . I gotta stop doing what I'm-a doing *now* . . . so that I can end up doing what I'm-a doing . . . *now?*"

Papa was not *against* working per se, but he was *for* a certain quality of working. Papa would say, *"Bisogno lavore—a piacere"* (It's important to work—as it pleases you)—as the creative impulse rises.

My mother remembers when she was about five, how *nice* it was to watch the three-decker being built. She told me: "All the big construction was done by Papa's friend, Carlo Cosmai. And then Papa did the inside work. I remember the long, narrow strips of beautiful wood he used for the wainscoting to decorate the main hallway on all the floors of the three-decker. I loved to watch the *way* he worked."

For Papa, working from love is not work. There is an ease, a flow, a joy. Papa walked, moved—measuredly. Some would say slowly, as if his body were speaking: "Whatever needs to get-a done, will get-a done . . . in its own time."

Let's be fair. This was a family with five children to feed and clothe.

"What do you mean—*a piacere*? We *need-a* da food on-a da table . . . *now.*" That was my grandmother—Nana—Marianina. And she could be scary.

All of the kids in the neighborhood were afraid of Marianina. Her house and yard were impeccable. Anywhere in Marianina's house, you could run your finger across the top of the doorframe without finding a trace of dust. Immaculate. Uncle Vito, mischievous son-in-law, caused havoc in the family one time when he picked up some outside dirt with his finger, ran it across the top of Marianina's doorframe, and asked, "What's this?"

Bottom line, Marianina worked hard inside the house, and sometimes she took jobs outside the house to make sure that the family got what they needed . . . *now*.

Nana was the pragmatist to Papa's visionary. And DeSantis family life was forged in the creative tension between the two.

But there is something else to consider when we talk about Papa and work. During that time (1910 to 1920), there were increasing numbers of agitations, strikes, and riots—to protest the horrific working conditions that existed all across the US.

There was violence on both sides:

- Anarchist bombings and attempted bombings.
- Unprovoked attacks against striking workers.
- In Ludlow, Colorado (1914), an unprovoked massacre of striking miners.
- In Lawrence, Massachusetts, during the Textile Strike (1912), marching women and their children were clubbed down by police. Other Massachusetts strikes happened in Plymouth and in Hopedale—right down the street from Worcester, where we lived.

There was spreading hysteria that decade. There was the Red Scare. Hundreds of radicals were captured. Arrests, deportations, false accusations of murder. In that climate, known anarchists were routinely blackballed. That was the tactic companies used to manage labor.

One day Papa went to look for work right in Worcester, a big manufacturing town. Shouldn't be so difficult.

The whole family became deeply concerned when, at the end of the day, Papa hadn't come back. "Where is he? Where could he be? What's going on?"

The unspoken questions were: "Was he speaking? Did anyone hear him? Were the police there?"

It so happened that someone in the family was walking on Elm Street where the Worcester Public Library was. When they looked through the library's plate glass windows, there was Papa, sitting at a long oak table. He'd spent the day reading. No job. The question remains—just plain lazy? Or blackballed?

It was 1920 and my mother was ten years old when Sacco and Vanzetti were indicted for robbery and murder. She told me, "Until then I used to like it when my father talked. His voice would go right through me. I absorbed his ideas and I would stick up for him. I wanted to be one of the *anarchisti*, too. We went to the parade and I sang with him, '*Viva l'anarchia e la libertà!*' But then I was very young and innocent."

She told me that as she got older, she became more afraid and began to argue with her father: "I hated it when he went too much with that crowd. Sometimes I was afraid he was more for them than for us. He wasn't so committed to the cause as some of those men—well, he was committed, but not a leader. I think he liked to listen to the speeches. Maybe he made some 'comments.' I don't know. Sometimes I wonder if he was arrested and I was too young to really grasp it."

She told me that by the time she was fifteen or sixteen she really told him off. "I didn't want him to wear that black flouncy tie anymore! It was a signal that you were an anarchist. People were getting arrested just for wearing that tie. In 1919, a man in Chicago was shot because he didn't take his hat off when they played "The Star Spangled Banner." I just didn't want him to talk about what he thought, how he felt, who his friends were. Even if he said a couple of words, it was bad . . . I was terrified that one night there would be banging at the door!"

My mother was seventeen when worldwide efforts to save Sacco and Vanzetti failed. On August 23, 1927 they were executed. And Edna St. Vincent Millay wrote: "Justice Denied in Massachusetts."

❧ Love ❧

Around that same time something else was happening in the DeSantis household. Four lovely daughters were blossoming and the boys noticed.

Now we know Papa believed in freedom. So that must have included *l'amore. Aah—l'amore.* Natural and free, consensual, no domination, no exploitation.

Here again is that creative tension in the family, between what we can hope for and what we can actually live out. *L'amore libero*, yes, but—the DeSantis girls? The rule was you became engaged first, and then you went out on a date—chaperoned by at least two sisters.

As for Papa himself. He loved. Something else I haven't told you about Papa's cellar. There was a pile of nudist colony magazines. I found out recently from cousin Frank that Papa actually introduced his male grandsons to his magazines. He taught that nudity was art. It was natural, and therefore beautiful in all its forms.

He would say, pointing to his magazine pictures, "See, she's beautiful, he's beautiful and she's beautiful and . . . you're beautiful. All . . . beautiful."

Papa even commissioned his oldest grandchild, my cousin Jim, to operate the projector he couldn't manage, so that together they could watch his nudist colony movies.

And Papa made art of his many magazine cutouts of beautiful nudes. He would carefully display them in his handcrafted picture frames that he had lying around his cellar workshop.

Papa went to Miami Beach each winter in his later years— even after our grandmother, Marianina, whom he'd outlived by twenty-five years, had died. Word came back that he was seeing a certain Canadian woman. One spring, Papa invited this Adrienne to come to Worcester. She spoke French. He spoke Italian. They had a few English words in common— that's it.

Papa sent a couple of his sons-in-law, Vito and Angelo, and a grandson, one of my cousins, Louis, to the Greyhound bus station to pick up Adrienne. When they arrived, they saw a very fashionably dressed, elegant woman standing there, cigarette holder in her hand, puffing à la Garbo. The three of them looked at each other and said, "No . . . *no way!*"

So they rode around the block, looking for someone else. The second time around, she was still the only one standing. "Can't be," they said, and they drove around for a third time.

Finally, they sent Louis out to check. "Is your name Adrienne by any chance?"

"*Oui.*"

There was a general furor among Luigi's children:

"I'm not going to let some hussy come into my house."

"How does it look to have your eighty-five-year-old father consorting with some strange woman?"

"If they can't talk to each other, what do they *do* when they're together?"

Only my mother welcomed Adrienne to dinner and dared to ask this lovely, sophisticated woman: "What do you see in my father?"

"He's a true *gentil*-man. He takes me to symphonies, to operas. He is a man of *culture*. We understand each other without speaking."

It seems there were others besides Adrienne. The only way we found out was because years later, we were having a DeSantis cousins get-together, and we began to reminisce about Papa Luigi.

Cousin Karen said, "I was at some big holiday party, when I heard a total stranger telling stories about a certain Master Luigi, a really elderly man who had built quite a reputation with women down in Florida, and had even gotten his younger brother, Emmanuele, to join him in his adventures. I went right up to this stranger, 'That's my grandfather you're talking about! Who are you and how do you know all this?'"

Mind you, at that time, Papa Luigi had been dead at least twelve years!

Karen then revealed to us that she was Papa's translator and scribe for letters coming back and forth from Adrienne in Canada. "Papa swore me to secrecy."

"Wait a minute," said yet another Cousin Louis, "that was *my* secret with Papa, but her name wasn't Adrienne, and she lived in Barbados."

At which point, Cousin Jim stood up. "I got you all beat. One winter I went to visit Papa in Florida. He told me not to tell anyone. I went to pick him up in the convertible I was driving to take him for a ride—a nice grandfather/grandson ride, I thought. He was with a woman. I opened the front door for both of them to get in the front seat with me. Papa starts, 'No, no. We go in-a back. You, put-a da roof down. We go in-a back.'

"'Papa,' I said, 'it's going to be cold with the top down.'

"'Noooo. *L'aria fresca.* Fresh-a air, nice. You put-a da roof down. We go in-a back.'

"How do you think I felt? I'm the chauffer while my grandfather is hugging and kissing in the back seat of an open convertible. I was twenty-five. He was eighty-five."

He wanted to be young. And he was!

In 1974 when Papa was ninety-five years old, he wrote to his just-married grandson and namesake, Louis DeSantis: "*Carrissimi sposi, VIVA L'AMORE. Sempre amore, amore.*" (Dearest newlyweds, LONG LIVE LOVE. Always love, love.) He wished them a son: *Luigino quarto generazione*—and then wrote: "*Così il mondo si sta cambiando e avremo più libertà.*"

(This way, the world will keep changing and there will be more freedom.)

❧ *A New Vision* ❧

As years went by, Papa spoke less and less about his ideas. But every once in a while he would make a remark and shake his head at injustice and closed-mindedness.

He lived a long, simple life, guided by his ideals, but mindful of the times in which he lived. Free yet practical.

So where am I now in the telling of Papa's story?

Ever present to my mother's fears—"Is it really okay to tell the story? Even now?"

One day I found some ragged pieces of paper on which Papa had scribbled lists and lists of names. Obviously, people he admired: Michelangelo, da Vinci, Toscanini, Verdi, Dante, Tolstoi, Pirandello, Hugo, Marconi, Fermi, Galileo, Einstein, Darwin. Then there was Cristo, San Francesco, Tommaso Jefferson, Abramo Lincoln, Eleanora Roosevelt.

He also listed important figures in the socialist, anarchist, libertarian movement. Some I knew: Marx, Engels, Lenin. Some I had to Google: Bakunin, Cafiero, Tresca, Galleani, Tommaso Campanella, Giordano Bruno.

I didn't have a strong reaction as I read about most of these historical figures. That is, until I looked up the sixteenth-century unorthodox thinkers Campanella (who was imprisoned for twenty-seven years) and Bruno (who was burned at the stake). They were described as martyrs to the cause of free thought. That's when something happened in my body. I felt fear take a shaking and gripping hold. You know, sometimes you don't get it until you *get* it!—like the orange.

I knew before that people get killed for speaking freely. But in that moment, the fear became what it must have been for my mother during the time of Sacco and Vanzetti—visceral and immediate. *People get killed.*

Martyrs to the cause of free thought—is that what happened to Sacco and Vanzetti?

Is that what the family feared could actually happen to Papa Luigi?

How many families besides my own lived in terror like that? How many still do?

And how many of those family fears—everything's dangerous, they're going to attack you outside, they're going to attack you inside—could find their roots during that period of our family history?

Fear like that can keep spreading, generalizing, in families. It's not only fear for your physical safety if you come out into the world to express yourself, but what about:

> ➢ FEAR that you will be rejected simply for being different, for having beliefs outside the mainstream.
> ➢ FEAR that who you are and what you believe will be reduced to some label and maybe a misunderstood one at that. In my grandfather's case, Italian anarchist could be, for some, the same as dangerous radical or bomb thrower. Yes, there were those who threw bombs, those who were extremely violent. But that's not the whole story by far. There's a distinction between what was *done* in the *name* of anarchism and anarchism itself. *No, no, no. Not any one of us is reducible to little boxes.*

> ➤ FEAR that you will be thought foolish, dismissed as Pollyannish, because what you want to say *is* so simple: *You're beautiful. It's all about LOVE. It's about people not bullying each other, not taking advantage. It's about laughing and crying together through this life, about having work and play be as one.*

Isn't it something how powerful stuff, like fears, gets passed down through the generations? All that time my ambivalence, my reticence about telling Papa's story, his philosophy, his way of being in the world, was about my mother's fear trapped in me.

Time to unravel the fear, time to use its fierce energy to step into courage, time to step out of that old program into greater degrees of freedom.

All through my teenage years, I used to have a recurring dream—really a nightmare. In it Papa Luigi was the gatekeeper for the family compound. He had a gate that he would arch open so all of his grandchildren could run through to go out and play. When it came time to return home, Papa would raise the arch and back we would come. But every time—before *I* could get back home—Papa slammed down the arch, and I would be stuck outside. *Why won't you let me come home, Papa? Why are you keeping me out, Papa?* I knew he loved me. It was a disturbing dream that I never understood at the time. Then I grew up and forgot about it.

But now when I think about my St. Louis reverie, and I see myself running through the Gateway Arch, I realize that my old nightmare has become a guiding vision.

I can see Papa's smiling face. I can hear his voice: "Stay out-a some more. You no have-a to run back-a home so soon. Go, be free. . . . Go, speak. Yes, home is-a nice, safe, but also is-a . . . too tight. No be 'fraid. *Mah*, you can be practical. *Coraggio.* Remember, courage means to speak-a you mind with all-a you heart. Some people will like, some people no like. Go, tell-a da story. Whadda you mean 'What's-a da story?' (*Phfufff.*) You *free*. Whatever story *you* want. Go, tell-a da story."

Well, Papa . . . looks like I just did!

And now I see my mother's face before me. "Mom . . . Mom, it's okay. I-I-I-just told the story. And it's really okay. Even now. Look, Ma, I'm still living out loud."

Thank you, Papa. Ti amo. *I love you.*

Papa Luigi with Bartolomeo Vanzetti, 1913.

The DeSantis Family, 1921.
Back: Papa Luigi;
Center Row: Bina, Nana Marianina, Maria, Jo;
Front Row: Artea, Libro.

PART II

LAUGHING OUT LOUD

3

To Laugh or Not to Laugh

To laugh or not to laugh? A conflict in me, informed by my parents, to assure that I would never lack having *stuff* to work on as I journey through life.

On one hand, there was my mother, who was sweet, serious, and easily given to tears. Her nickname was *Maria la piangente,* Maria the weeper. She was a proper woman—always thinking about what was the right way to respond in any situation. I remember one time when I was laughing full out, my mother said, "Don't laugh so hard. When you laugh like that your mouth is wide open and your body gets all twisted. You don't look good."

Oh, when we laugh, we have to think about looking good! That's when, as my mother's daughter, I learned to ha-ha-ha "nicely," which means not too boisterously and only from the neck up with lips parted slightly. Alternatively known as fake laughing.

On the other hand, there was my father, who was ever ready to see the comic side of any situation. There was nothing fake about my dad's laugh. He never worried about how his features would distort or how raucous the sounds were when he laughed. His laugh was like a merry-go-round that invited you to hop on and ride with him.

My dad could completely bypass thinking. You could say he'd be "out of his mind" and laugh for any reason whatsoever. Or no reason at all! I remember one day sitting next to a teacher who was talking to a group of other students. I couldn't hear what they were saying, but at some point they all started laughing. I started laughing, too. The teacher startled me when he turned abruptly and asked, "Why are *you* laughing?"

"I don't know. I need a reason to laugh?" I didn't know I needed a reason. I'm my father's daughter. You just laugh.

Back to the one hand, if there had been a gene for "can't get jokes," my mother would have possessed it without question. For example, I once handed her a lighthearted book I thought she might enjoy. She read the title: "*Old Is Not a Four-Letter Word.*" She said, "I know *that*. Do I have to read the whole book to find that out?"

One day when I thought my mother was pushing herself too hard, I asked, "Are you rushing, Mom?"

"NO," she answered.

My husband Bob playfully interjected, "She's not Russian. She's Italian."

"Mom did you understand what Bob said?"

"Italians don't rush?" she laughed. "Maybe that's true. They can be slowpokes."

Another time while enjoying lunch together in a restaurant, my mother said, "Look at those people laughing at us. What do we care? Let's pretend we're comedians and we're doing a good job. They're laughing."

I burst out laughing, amazed at the possibility that my mother was beginning to get her groove on.

She looked at me, puzzled. "What's so funny about that? I don't get it."

Trying to help my Mom "get the joke" was a lost cause. Have you ever had to take ten minutes to explain a joke that took five seconds to tell? After about five minutes, all meaning has disappeared. You're trapped in a conversation, trying to get back on track. Meanwhile, she's made several loose associations that blur the possibility of your finding any way back. That's when you smile and remember how much you love her.

Back to the other hand, if there had been a gene for comedic proclivities, my dad would have possessed it in abundance. He got jokes, told jokes, embodied jokes.

He was free to clown without hesitation, as when he would pick up a trumpet or other instrument he couldn't play, and regale an appreciative family with cacophony rather than music, or when he pranced around pretending to be an elite soccer player, while the family's children giggled and egged on their favorite playful Uncle Nicky.

My mother, my father . . . both have always lived in me. Life was admittedly more fun whenever my father bubbled up. But I had a problem with that—the fear of not being taken seriously, of being dismissed as frothy and frivolous, a lightweight.

I wanted more than levity. I wanted profundity, not pro-fun-dittiness, but something to demonstrate how deep and meaningful I could be. *I know,* I thought. *I'll get a Ph.D.!*

And I did . . . and I received a benefit beyond what ordinarily comes with having a doctorate. Whenever my father bubbles up in me, people are less likely to say, "Such a fool, so ridiculous," without adding, "*she's* got a Ph.D.?"

However, my dismissive attitude toward levity shifted with time as scientific studies began to demonstrate the beneficial effects of humor and laughter on health and happiness. There are physiological benefits that have been well documented. Genuine laughter is a cardio exercise that oxygenates the body and the brain, reducing stress and strengthening the immune system. Norman Cousins likened it to inner jogging.

There are psychological and emotional benefits, too. Genuine laughter releases endorphins, chemicals naturally manufactured in the brain that elevate mood. Even genuine smiles, which engage the muscles around the mouth and the eyes, were found to release endorphins, unlike fake smiles, which engage only the muscles around the mouth.

Feel-good endorphins help create a positive mental state that can give us hope and optimism during those inevitable, trying, and painful times of life.

Dealing first with breast cancer and then bladder cancer were especially difficult times for me. They were easier to handle whenever spontaneous moments of genuine laughter erupted. With every burst of laughter, the universe that I was inhabiting the moment before expanded. Cancer, while still there, now occupied a much smaller corner of my universe, and I was freer and more able to bear its weight.

My appreciation of laughter grew when, in the mid-nineties, I was introduced to the work of Dr. Mardan Kataria, a medical doctor from India. Dr. Kataria developed Laughter Yoga, whereby you don't have to wait for those infrequent moments of spontaneous laughter. He initiates laughter as a body exercise in a group, and with eye contact and childlike playfulness, it soon turns into genuine and contagious laughter. Laughing for no reason. Acting happy can actually make you happy. How many are the ways to keep those endorphins flowing?

Clearly, laughter is healing. It has weight, substance, value. It's not simply a laughing matter. Ethologist Konrad Lorenz said, "We don't take humor seriously enough."

Seeing that juxtaposition of the words "humor" and "serious" within a single phrase brought a smile to my lips and a new way of relating to those words not as oppositional but as richly related.

Ancient Greek masks of comedy and tragedy—one laughing, one weeping—remind me of the adage, "No comedy. No tragedy." We laugh. We cry. That's life! Golda Meier said, "Those who don't know how to weep with their whole heart don't know how to laugh either."

And how about the expression "they laughed until they cried?" Comedian Sid Caesar once said, "Crying and laughing are the same emotion. If you laugh too hard, you cry. And vice versa." Interestingly, it's been demonstrated that the same set of muscles are engaged in both. Laughing and crying—at once different and the same.

When I think now of my dear parents (who will forgive me for this over-simplification—one humorous, one serious, one who laughs, one—not so much), the tension between their different ways of being doesn't live in me as it did when I was younger, because now I see them both as part of a whole.

These words from Virginia Woolfe stay with me: "The beauty of the world has two edges, one of laughter, one of anguish."

Thank you, Mom, thank you, Dad, for masterfully demonstrating both sides of the beauty of the world, so that I could learn about holding both at the same time . . . and dancing between the two. Knowing that whether I'm waltzing or jitterbugging, I'm in the Dance of Life.

4

Wander in Wonder

D id you ever wonder where the wonder went?

Oh, for the love of being young again!
When we're kids every moment is fresh and new.
We're open, curious, filled with wonder—that sense of
*   magic, that wide-eyed curiosity that looks out upon the*
*   world, always ready to be astonished.*

We get older. Things change. Self-consciousness kicks in.
How do I look?
What are they going to think of me?
Am I doing the right thing?

We're not in the moment anymore!
We're lost in our heads.
Spontaneity gone, we get stuck in routines.
Doing what's expected, what's safe (we think).
Acting from inside the boxes we've created for ourselves.

But no matter how much I age (and I notice I keep doing
*   that), there's always the call to break free of same old,*
*   same old.*
Just for the love of doing something different.
The love of shaking up expectations.

The love of being present . . . moment to moment.
And then watching with open and curious eyes what
wondrous thing might show up just around the next
corner.

❧ The Plot is Hatched ❧

Take a stroll back with me to 1992. I'm having lunch at a trendy restaurant on Beacon Hill in Boston right near the State House with some of my female cousins—blood cousins, cousins of the heart, all *family*—Cousin Karen, Cousin Dona, Cousin Rita, and me.

We're having so much fun at this luncheon that we agree, "We've got to get together more often! Even though we all live *so far apart* . . . Worcester, Mass., Shrewsbury, Mass., Southboro, Mass., and Wellesley, Mass."

"I know!" says Cousin Karen. "Let's plan a Cousin's Day in Boston. We'll include the guys."

"Let's do something special!" says Cousin Dona.

"I know," says Cousin Rita. "How about a harbor cruise? We'll take one of those boats docked next to the aquarium."

"That's a plan," says I. "We'll do it."

We continue our lunch and the conversation turns to old times, high school proms, and the dresses we wore in the fifties.

"Not fair," says Cousin Karen, who is a bit younger than the rest of us. "You guys got to wear those big tulle gowns with all that nylon netting and all those crinolines underneath."

"I still have my high school junior prom dress," I add in passing.

"I know someone who saved *all* of her prom dresses," says Cousin Rita.

"*What if*," Cousin Karen exclaims, eyes wide open, "for our Cousin's Day boat ride in Boston Harbor, we *all* wore prom dresses?"

"Come on! No way!" The three of us begin to giggle.

"Menopausal women in high-school prom dresses?"

"Really, come *on!*"

"No, *really!*" says Cousin Karen. "I'd love to borrow one of those big tulle dresses."

"I could borrow one, too," says Cousin Rita.

That's when I hear myself say, "I guess I could bring mine down from the attic."

"Oh *puh-lease*," says Cousin Dona. "I don't want to wear a prom dress for a daytime boat ride in Boston Harbor. I still have my old *wedding* dress! If I take a little out on the side, I can make it fit. I want to be the bride!"

We break out in gales of laughter at the thought of women our age being so outrageous. We envision a Miss Havisham bride in her decaying and tattered wedding dress trailed by three ragtag bridesmaids, as they step off a Boston pier onto some rickety dingy.

"*Ooooh*," wails Cousin Rita, "we're going to look so beautiful on the boat, and I'm going to be the *most* beautiful. I want to be the belle of all."

By now we're howling with laughter and trying not to fall out of our chairs. When we see people in the restaurant giving us *that look*, we just laugh more!

"Let's not tell the guys," says Cousin Karen gleefully. "We'll keep it a secret! They'll never call each other to ask, 'What are you going to wear on the cruise?' It'll be . . . 'Surprise!'"

We leave the restaurant convulsing still. Standing at a corner on Beacon Hill, we can't stop! We're doubled over, holding our sides, crossing our legs. But now, as people pass by, instead of giving us *that look*, many of them smile back at us. There's a twinkling in their eyes that connects us to each other.

We look up at the State House and, out of the upstairs office windows, people are leaning out, laughing and waving back at us.

"Who are those people?" we ask each other.

"Do you know?"

"I don't know?"

"Do *you* know?"

Nobody knows.

"Maybe they're cousins."

Driving home after our lunch, it's great fun just *thinking* about doing something unexpected—outside the box. Imagination alone creates full-bodied, guffawing laughter, which leads to immediate connection with others.

What could possibly happen? What other surprises might be in store if we actually followed through? Saying is one thing. Doing is something else.

❧ *Is It Really Happening?* ❧

The day arrives. Eight cousins going to Boston for our one o'clock boat ride in the Harbor. Five cousins will be going directly to the pier from Worcester. Cousin Karen in Southborough will pick me up in Wellesley. We'll pick up my husband, Bob, who works in Brookline, and the three of us will join the other five at the pier.

Not knowing who will be wearing what for this event, I go to the attic, bring down my high school junior prom dress, change into it, and wait for Cousin Karen. She calls from her bulky car phone (cell phones have not yet arrived on the scene).

"I know I'm late," says a harried Cousin Karen. "I'm coming as fast as I can."

"I'll meet you outside to save time," says I. "I'll be standing at the end of the driveway."

Get the picture: It's midday, Wellesley, Massachusetts. A quiet staid neighborhood, cute Colonial houses, manicured lawns (except ours). I'm standing at the end of the driveway, virtually in the street. It's the early nineties and I'm wearing my 1953 yellow, strapless, many tiered, tulle-netted prom dress, topped with a little white cashmere sweater and its detachable fur collar and rhinestone cuff links. I add sheer nylon gloves, rhinestone earrings, and matching necklace. I'm perched on three-inch, sandal-strapped high heels.

And so, there is at least one bridesmaid.

Finally, Cousin Karen swings around the corner and all I can see in the front seat of the car is her big red curly hair and blue tulle sprouting everywhere.

Two bridesmaids!

Cousin Karen pulls up, jumps out of the car, and says, "I know it's late, but I need help."

The strapless dress she's borrowed is *way* too big on top. I run to get some safety pins and try to fix it so it won't fall off. All the while, she's alternately hoisting the troublesome top and flicking the blue tulle bottom—hoisting and flicking, hoisting and flicking. She loves to flick, because it's her first time in a puffy tulle dresses. On one of the flicks, I notice her feet.

"You're wearing sneakers!" I proclaim.

She looks at me, "What do you think, I'm *stupid?* We're going on a BOAT!"

Oh, stupid me! How could I forget?

We pile into the car. Her blue tulle takes up the whole front seat, so I get in the back with my yellow tulle. Next we're off to get Bob in Brookline. I call Bob on the car phone.

"We're running late, honey. We don't have time to stop. Wait outside and watch for us. You'll see blue and yellow tulle. Don't ask questions."

We collect Bob, dressed in his business attire, jacket, shirt, tie, pants, dress shoes. He jumps in the back seat with me.

"What do you think?" we ask.

He shrugs. "I married into this clan a long time ago, and I still don't get it."

We speed down Huntington Avenue. Cousin Karen is weaving, cutting in and out of traffic, sliding on the trolley tracks, clipping the median strip. We're not going to make launch time.

With one hand on the wheel, Cousin Karen picks up the car phone: "Please operator, this is an emergency. Please put my call through to the Bay Harbor Cruise Company. . . . Hello, hello, Bay Harbor Cruise Company! Listen, we're scheduled on the one p.m. boat. And you *have* to hold the boat. . . . No, no, no, you don't understand. We're in a terrible predicament. We're part of a wedding party and they can't get married without us. We have two of the bridesmaids and . . . *um* . . . *um* . . . the photographer here. We're on the way. Please, *please.* Hold the boat!"

She spins her head around to address the two of us in the back seat: "She can't hold the boat."

To the phone: "If you can't hold the boat, would you at least look outside to see if there's a bride and a bridesmaid?"

To the back seat: "She's going outside to look."

To the phone: "Hello, yes, yes."

To the back seat: "She thinks she sees them."

To the phone: "Uh-huh, uh-huh."

To the back seat: "She sees the bride!"

To the phone: "Uh-huh, uh-huh."

To the back seat: "She wants to know if the bridesmaid is wearing teal!"

Teal? She's asking *us*, if the bridesmaid is wearing teal? Until that moment we had no idea whether there would even be a third bridesmaid, let alone what color she chose.

Now we know that our wedding party is complete. There will be a bride in white—and three simple tulles/tools in yellow, blue, and teal.

Finally, we get to the dock.

"Sorry," the attendant says, "I couldn't hold the boat for you, but they go out every half hour. And your bridal party said they would be waiting for you next door in the terrace lounge at the Long Wharf Marriott."

❦ *The Wedding Begins* ❧

We ride the escalator up to the terrace lounge overlooking the sparkling harbor. We hug, we kiss. We guffaw at the sight of us. We can't believe that all four of us have gone from the talk to the walk.

There's cousin Dona, the bride, resplendent in white, with crown, veil, train, dangling earrings, necklace, and paper flower bouquet. She gives each of her bridesmaids a little gift from the back of an old jewelry box—recycled clip-on earrings. Cousin Rita, in teal, has really outdone everybody. Bows galore. She's the only one with a headpiece. Big bows made of teal taffeta and white lace perched tentatively on one side of her head. Her matching bouquet looks like a big white bird ready to take flight. No *little* fur collar. Cousin Rita brought a full mink stole. But not *just* the mink. For good measure, she brought along a fox pelt—like the ones you see in the movies of the thirties and forties. Women with a whole fox draped on their shoulders—with head, tail, and paws dangling. Cousin Rita said she would be the best dressed. The belle of all. And she was!

The men—another story. We already have Bob, the . . . photographer. And now we're joined by my Cousin Lou, my Other Cousin Lou, and my Other-Other Cousin Lou.

My first Cousin Lou—Cousin Dona's husband—doesn't miss a beat when he sees his wife come down from their bedroom dressed for a one-hour boat ride in her old wedding dress. He runs up to get a bow tie and cummerbund to go with his khakis and sneakers.

My Other Cousin Lou, from the moment he lays eyes on us, can't stop laughing, and that's what he does—all day long.

As for my Other-Other Cousin Lou, he comes dressed in splendid boat attire including nautical sweatshirt and those special rubber-soled shoes to keep him from slipping on the deck if it gets wet. Because his good Italian mother taught him the essential lessons of life, he also carries a waterproof gym bag with a full set of dry clothes. So what if all this boat does is circle the placid waters of Boston's inner harbor? You never know when a big wave will come crashing over the railing and inundate you completely. You have to be prepared!

Notably, this Other-Other Cousin Lou doesn't laugh at all. He just stands back, arms folded, gym bag in hand, shaking his head and glumly repeating over and over: "I don't know you people."

By the time we complete our wedding cocktail hour on the terrace, we miss a couple more boats rides. In the spirit of being in the moment and curious about what else might await us around the next corner, we decide we'll simply stroll through Little Italy's North End. At a minimum, we'll eat well.

As we ride the escalator down and walk through the Marriott lobby, my Other-Other Cousin Lou, gym bag still in hand, following a few paces behind, calls out to anyone he encounters: "I don't know those people. I really don't know those people. *I don't know them.*"

When we step out of the Marriott, we're struck by the beauty and the brilliance of the day. We're in Cristoforo Colombo Park, with its vine-covered arched walkways to the left, and Boston Harbor to the right. Glistening boats that we could almost touch. A dream setting. We could never have arranged a more ideal backdrop for a . . . wedding ceremony.

"Let's do it," says Cousin Karen. "Line up everybody. Lou, stand next to your wife, the bride!"

Cousin Dona says, "I married him once. Do I have to marry him again?"

"Okay, Bob, you're the only one with a tie. You get to be the groom. Who's got the ring?"

Cousin Rita takes off a rhinestone clip earring. "This can work perfectly."

We're all set, except who's going to perform the ceremony? No brainer. My Other-Other Cousin Lou with the gym bag is actually a judge. "How about it, Judge?"

"Did you forget?" he asks. "I don't associate with people like you. And anyway, I'm not dressed appropriately."

Then the judge points to Cousin Rita's mink stole and says, "I'll take the mink. You can keep the fox."

He drapes the mink over his shoulders and begins: "Dearly Beloved, we are gathered here on this glorious and sparkling day, in this magnificent historic park with the ivy swaying and the birds tweeting, with the clear blue sky above and the shimmering water below, with the boats bobbing up and down, and all these tourists looking at us as if we're mad—and *we are*—to marry these two ridiculous people in the sight of their even more ridiculous entourage, and for this, dear Lord, we ask your forgiveness. I now pronounce you—whatever you are."

And we smile, as Japanese tourists and a young couple from Iowa snap our pictures. As for the mink stole, once my Other-Other Cousin Lou put it on his shoulders, there it would stay for the rest of the day. Everywhere that Louie went, the mink stole and gym bag were sure to go.

❧ Where's the Bride? ❧

Ceremony over, we wander along Atlantic Avenue, still open to whatever else the day will bring. A red motorcycle, racing down the street, comes to a complete stop right in front of us. It seems people are drawn to us like magnets.

This stranger on the motorcycle in his leather jacket shouts out to the bride, "Hey, wanna go for a ride?"

"Sure!" says Cousin Dona, who lifts up her gown and straddles the red bike.

Next thing we see is her white train . . . dragging on the ground . . . veil flapping in the wind. Around the first bend, she disappears. We've lost the bride.

Cousin Rita in teal freaks out. She runs up to Cousin Lou, the real husband, and screams into his face, "What are you . . . *crazy?* You let your wife go with a stranger on a motorcycle? He could be a serial killer. She's gonna get *murdered!*"

"Don't worry, Rita," easy-going Cousin Lou says, "he's got a Madonna on the front of the motorcycle."

"And *that's* your proof he's not a serial killer? Who puts a Madonna on a motorcycle?" With hysteria mounting she adds, "Do you know? *Do you know?* I don't know, but you don't know *either!* She's gone! . . . *Oooh, my gawd!* What are you gonna tell your kids?"

The bride does come back, and thankfully, she's none the worse for wear except for the extra dirt on her train. We spend some time schmoozing and getting acquainted with the motorcycle man. He could have been another cousin.

◦∘ *Are We in an Episode of The Sopranos?* ∘◦

We're beginning to get hungry and wander up one of the little side streets in the North End aiming toward Hanover Street. On the narrow sidewalk we pass a couple of men sitting on hard chairs on either side of a small doorway.

They, like so many others that day, call out to us, "*Eh.* How ya doin'? Whatcha doin'?"

"We just had a wedding. There's the bride and groom and we're the wedding party."

"Yeah? Wanna come in?"

"What do you mean?"

"We got a social club in here. Good spot for a wedding. You can have a drink. You can have a dance."

Why not? We walk into a big dark room. A few tables and chairs on the sides. Four or five guys hanging around. A bar in one corner and a jukebox in the other. One of the guys near the bar raises his chin and tilts his head in a "come ova he-ah" motion to my Other Cousin Lou.

Whispering, he asks, "Youz guyz Feds?"

"*Feds?* Us? Feds? Would Feds stoop to this? We don't think so!" we say as we hoist and flick multi-colored layers of tulle.

"You're okay," the man in the corner says. "Joey, a round of drinks on the house and put money in the jukebox." Before we know it, Dean Martin starts singing "That's Amore."

"It's the first dance! Bride, groom, come on!" *La-la-la, la-la-la.* "Okay, next dance, Let's go . . . yellow, blue, teal! Come on . . . Lou, Lou, Lou! Everybody dance!" *La-la-la, la-la-la, la-la-la, la-la-la,* that's *amore. Sempre amore.* Forever love.

We pay for the second round of drinks. The man in the corner says "eight bucks." Not bad for the bar tab at a wedding.

❧ *If It's an Italian Wedding, We Have to Eat* ❧

Suddenly, we're really hungry. "Where could we go to eat?" we ask.

One of the guys at the social club says, "Go to Mateo's around the corner. Good food. You'll like it. He's my cousin."

Eh—of course. What else!

We set out for Mateo's, continuing to draw attention. People staring at us ask questions. "Who are you? What are you supposed to be?"

At first we attempt some kind of answer, like, "We just love weddings so much that whenever we get together we have to have one."

When they ask, "Is this a movie? Are we going to be in a movie?"

All we come up with is, "Do you see any cameras?"

Then we realize it's more fun to hear what *they* have to say. We ask, "What do *you* think's going on?"

Whatever their answer, we reply enthusiastically, "That's right!" because now we get the picture. We're a living, strolling Rorschach ink blot.

However we're perceived is completely up to the beholder. Do some see us as silly or foolish . . . childish? Do others see us as enlightened or joyful . . . childlike? Maybe both? Or maybe neither?

Makes you think . . . for any of us . . . whenever we look at each other, what do we see?

Who's out there . . . really?

We find our way to Cousin Mateo's place, a tiny restaurant with a few small tables off to each side—all occupied. The one lone table in the middle—available. It's a table for eight. Just waiting for us? As we take our places at the bridal table, the other restaurant patrons start to applaud. They toast with us, feast with us.

Strangers become family. Just like that—you guessed it—more cousins.

❧ *Cannoli at the End* ☙

When it's time for dessert, we meander across the street to a Hanover Street cafe because, as anyone "in the know" knows, in the North End, you don't have dessert in the same place you had your entree. We pull together a couple of bistro tables and chairs, sit down, and order our cannoli with espresso.

Someone, maybe the manager, approaches us and says, "I want to show you something special."

We've been to this cafe many times before, but nobody ever singled us out in this way.

"Come," he says, directing us to a lower level in the cafe that I never knew existed, "a special place for special people."

"But wait," he says, leading us down to an even lower level ". . . a *more* special place." Here everything has a shrine-like feeling. As he points to different chairs in the room, he whispers, "Over there sat Enrico Caruso. And over there, Arturo Toscanini."

We take it all in and I swear I detect the smell of old cigar smoke and heavy red wine that lives in these walls. After we thank him for our special treat, we go back upstairs, sip our espresso, and finish our cannoli.

Suddenly the day is over. Time to go. We hug, kiss, say our goodbyes, and shake our heads in amazement.

↜ *Epilogue* ↝

Something extraordinary happened that day. From beginning to end, a magical experience. We were young again—in the way that makes a difference—young at heart. We had dared to step out of the box of what's expected. We stayed in the moment, present to whatever showed up.

For sure, joy and laughter showed up. "At the height of laughter," said Jean Houston, "the universe is flung into a kaleidoscope of new possibilities."

New possibilities did show up . . . for connection.

Throughout the day, usual barriers among strangers fell away. Laughing together created instant relationships and everybody we met turned out to be like family. Yes, Victor Borge, we agree: "Laughter is the shortest distance between two people."

It was an amazing day, which lives still as a touchstone to remember:

Break the mold.
Stay present.
Stay open.
Keep laughing.
Collect Cousins.

PART III

LOVING OUT LOUD

5

Reminiscences of Love

It was three weeks before her 100th birthday that my mother died. What an amazingly long life, considering how much of it she spent being so fearful of . . . *everything*. The next tragedy always lurked, and death was the inevitable result for her children, her loved ones, and of course, herself. She was sure she'd never see me go to kindergarten, graduate from high school, get married.

"*Ooh*," she would moan, "I'll never see my grandchildren."

She lived to see it all, even her five *great*-grandchildren.

❧ ❧

My mother was eighty-six and my father eighty-eight when they came to live with Bob and me. It was 1996, and it was time. My dad died only six months later. A sad time. "Oh my Nick. I miss him terribly," she would say.

At my dad's funeral, a friend of the family, offering condolences to my mother, said, "You and Nick loved each other so much."

"How did you know?" my mother asked curiously. "He was never affectionate in public."

"I always knew," she said. "You could just see it."

Well, they had been pretty inseparable. Others who knew them would say, "Mary-and-Nick is one word." She was always on his arm. "He was my pocketbook," she'd say. And if you know anything about a woman of her generation's relationship to pocketbooks, you'll understand what that means. I've heard that Queen Elizabeth is never without a pocketbook dangling from her arm, as she moves from one room to another within Buckingham Palace.

It had been thirty-eight years since I last lived with my mother—not since 1958, when I married Bob. Now she and I would have the luxury of time together, time for leisure conversation, time for memories, time to hear facts and glean subtleties never known before.

She reminisced about how she and my dad met. When she was fourteen, she was allowed to go to dances at the Italian-American club—chaperoned by her mother, of course.

He was sixteen, and as they used to say back then—"fresh off the boat." He really couldn't speak much English, and he was an "older man." So when he asked my mother to dance, my grandmother shooed him away.

It wasn't until four years later, when my mother was eighteen, that he asked her to dance again. Over the years, she watched him become more American and turn into such a wonderful dancer that all the girls wanted to be his partner.

In the custom of the day, he motioned to her from across the dance floor by raising his arm and waving an index finger that meant . . . *the next dance?*

She nodded, timidly but surely.

She waited, excitedly, anxiously. But when the next dance began, instead of being with her, he was holding someone else in his arms. She was crushed.

She wondered: "Is this his revenge for having been refused a dance four years before? Or is it because I'm skinny and dark, and I have an overbite, and my nose is a little big, and my eyes are too sunken in their sockets, and my legs are bowed?"

She felt ugly inside and figured how you feel inside must be how you really look.

"How could he like me?" she thought. "Not four years ago, not now."

But when the next dance began, he came to her, and took her in his arms.

She spoke shyly, "I thought you said the 'next' dance."

"No," he said, "I had *two* fingers up—that meant the dance *after* the next one." She relaxed a bit and let his smooth, gliding steps slowly take her away.

At that point in the story, my mother looked at me and said, "He wanted me when I was fourteen. I never believed that. I believe it now."

"Oh, my Nick was wonderful," she sighed. "I miss his love, his funniness. It was happiness just to be with him." She went on, "For sixty-three years we were married. My life was full of heartaches, so many hard and sad things, but he could make my heartaches almost be nothing. He made me laugh. He was such a comedian.

"You know, it's funny. I love him in my heart more—now. When he was alive, we used to bicker a lot. Sometimes we would stay mad at each other for days. We wouldn't speak to each other, except when the kids or the extended family were there. Everything would look normal until the minute they left. Then . . . nothing. But the cold shoulder never lasted more than a week, because Saturday night was always 'make-up' night.

"We used to have the same kind of argument . . . over and over again. He'd come home from work, and I'd be so happy to see him, because I missed him during the day. But after ten minutes it would start again.

"He'd say something and then I'd say, 'What did you say that for?'

"'I didn't say that,' he'd say.

"'Then I don't know what you're talking about,' I'd say.

"'Sixty years and you still don't know what I'm talking about?' he'd say.

"'Sixty years and I never knew what you were talking about,' I'd say.

"'That's because you never listened to me,' he'd say.

"'When did you ever listen to *me* all these years?' I'd say.

"'Okay, I'm not going to talk anymore,' he'd say.

"'Good,' I'd say.

"'Good! Good! You don't want me to talk anymore? I know, you want me dead. All right, I'm going to jump in Lake Quinsigamond and drown!' he'd say, if it were summer. Or if it were winter, he'd say, 'I'm going out in the snow without a coat and they'll find me frozen to death in the street.'

"'What?' I'd say. 'Now you want me to feel sorry for *you*? Who's going to feel sorry for *me*? You'll be dead and then what am I supposed to do?'"

She paused . . . her voice softened.

"But that's all gone—and now—all that's left is—I just love the guy."

I used to love it whenever my mother reminisced, got that wistful look in her eyes, and began to sing her favorite old Italian love song, *"Come un sogno d'or"* . . . Like a golden dream.

And now I grow wistful remembering a time when they were both living with me. They had gotten into some variation of the old Mary-and-Nick-bickering routine. He shuffled off to the living room. She sat and sulked in the kitchen.

It wasn't very long before he shuffled back, leaned over the back of her chair, and whispered in her ear. "Mae, don't you know? Don't you know how much I love you? You're the only one for me always."

She looked up, "Yes, Nick, me, too. You're the only man I

Mary (Maria) and Nick (Nicola) visiting Italy in 1947.
Nicola's first visit to see his family, twenty-three years after leaving at age sixteen.

could be with. Every other man was wrong. I think we were born together, Nick." And then they cried and held each other. And I was there, but they never saw me.

Engagement picture of Mary and Nick, 1933.

Mary and Nick in 1988.

6

Now We're in a Play

In 2001, my dear friend Riva told me she would be submitting a ten-minute play to The Actors Theatre of Louisville for the following season. "Why don't you write one, too?" she suggested.

"Me, write a play?" I'd never even considered that to be a form of creative expression for me.

But then I thought, *Why not? I've got absolutely nothing to lose, right? I'm free.* "Some people will like, some people no like."

And so I wrote and submitted my one and only play. Surprisingly, the Actors Theatre of Louisville acknowledged *It's Your Bid* as one of 100 finalists from 1,500 entries in their ten-minute play competition in 2002.

It's Your Bid depicts an actual card game conversation I had with my mother while she was still living with us. My dad had died five years earlier and soon she would be off to her "next adventure" at St Patricks Manor.

And now . . . curtain up.

It's Your Bid

a ten-minute play

[Lights up on a kitchen table. MARIA, 91 years old and in a wheelchair is playing bridge with her 65-year-old daughter, HELENA. MARIA and HELENA are trying to play all four hands. They have devised a strategy whereby each one bids for the imaginary partner of the other. MARIA, sitting in the North position (upstage), finishes dealing out the cards. HELENA sits in the West position.]

HELENA
Your deal, so what do you bid?

MARIA
*Hmm—uh—*I pass.

HELENA
And my partner?

MARIA
(Picks up and arranges the cards on her left or East position and bids)
Hmm, well . . . *uh* . . . one heart.

HELENA
(Picks up and arranges the cards on her right or South position and bids)
Let's see. Okay . . . I say two clubs.

MARIA

Don't say, "*I* say two clubs." Say, "*Your partner* says two clubs." Don't mix me up.

HELENA

All right . . . you passed, *my partner* said . . .
> *(Forgetting)*
. . What did my partner say?

MARIA

One heart.

HELENA

> *(Reviewing the bidding)*
Okay.
> *(Points to MARIA)*
Pass for you.
> *(Points to the empty chair opposite her)*
One heart for your partner, I mean *my* partner.
> *(Points to the empty chair to her right)*
I said two clubs over here. I mean *your* partner said two clubs. And now,
> *(Points to herself)*
I pass. Okay?

MARIA

Okay.
> *(Pauses; sighs deeply)*
I think I want to go to the psychiatrist again.

HELENA

Why? What's happening?

MARIA

I have to tell the psychiatrist that there's a voice in my head talking to me.

HELENA

What's this voice saying to you?

MARIA

It says that I've had a wonderful life, even though I've always had so many worries and fears. I keep hearing this in my head all the time. Somebody is talking in there.

HELENA

It's called "talking-to-yourself-in-your-head." Everybody does it.

MARIA

Really? I thought I was the only one.

HELENA

No such luck.

MARIA

(Taking a long hard look at the cards in her hand)
Okay. It's my bid, right? *Umm* . . . three clubs.

HELENA

All right, you and your partner got the bid for three clubs. . . .

(Pauses)
So who said clubs first? You or your partner?

MARIA

You said it first, but you were my partner.

HELENA

So we gotta switch.
(HELENA switches both sets of hands and gives South hand to MARIA)
Here's your hand.

MARIA

I didn't see this hand before.

HELENA

Because it's the one *I* had when I was your partner.

MARIA

Oh yeah, that's right.
(Pauses)
Now who's the dummy?

HELENA

The dummy's over here.
(HELENA picks up the dummy hand on her right and lays it out for MARIA)
Okay.
(Pointing to the hand across from her in the East position)
Now my partner *over there* has to lead.

(Picks up hand in the East position)
But I'm going to move my partner next to me now so I don't
have to keep reaching across the table.
(HELENA plays a card from the hand in her hand)

MARIA
So. . . .
(Playing a dummy card)
Now I play the dummy.

HELENA
(Playing a card from her own hand)
My turn.

MARIA
(Picking up trick #1)
My trick!
*(MARIA and HELENA keep playing throughout the
scene; MARIA will win all the tricks but one)*

MARIA
Nick was so good at cards. My poor Nick. . . . For sixty-three
years that man listened to me. . . . What other man would listen
all night to my worries?

HELENA
And he didn't even worry about how much you worried.

MARIA
I don't remember. Why?

HELENA

He would say, "It's okay. She's okay. She can worry. If she stops worrying, I won't know who she is."

(Pauses)

And he didn't want to lose you.

MARIA

(Nodding, reminiscing)

There was nobody else for me—nobody better looking, no better person, no better dancer. And he always made me laugh. He was a real Charlie Chaplin . . . or maybe Lou Costello. *(Chuckling)* The first time we saw Bud Abbott and Lou Costello in the movies, your father couldn't stop laughing for three days.

(MARIA picks up winning trick #2)

HELENA

(Looking sad suddenly)

MARIA

(Always checking on her daughter)

What's the matter? You look sad. Why are you sad now?

HELENA

I'm remembering how much fun he was. I miss him. I'm sad.

MARIA

You're educated. How can you get over that now? . . . Do you want to go to the psychiatrist?

HELENA

No . . . I don't want to go to the psychiatrist. . . . I don't have to get over it. Education doesn't matter. I'm just sad.

MARIA

All right . . . let's *both* be sad now.

HELENA

No . . . no-no-no-no. I'll be sad when I'm sad . . . and you'll be sad when you're sad.

MARIA
(Pausing to think)
Yeah, one time I was sad and *you* weren't.

HELENA

Yes, and one time you didn't give *me* a sweater when *you* were cold. . . .
(Picking up card)
I win this trick.
*(HELENA picks up winning trick #3; HELENA and
MARIA start to play the next trick)*

MARIA

What shall I say to the psychiatrist when I go?

HELENA

Say whatever you want.

MARIA

Should I tell him that I keep getting those same old fears over and over? I don't want to crab about my life. The doctor doesn't want to hear that.

(MARIA picks up winning trick #4)

HELENA

(Gradually speaking louder and faster)

Now you're worried about what the *doctor* wants to hear? Are you the doctor, now? Are you the doctor who's going to take care of the doctor, so he doesn't have to hear what you think he doesn't want to hear? What do you want to go to the doctor for if *you're* going to be the doctor?

MARIA

You don't have to get so loud. Okay, I'll tell the doctor. I'll crab. I have to say the same things. I'll tell him . . . I'm afraid I'm going to get sick. I'm afraid I'm going to go crazy.

HELENA

How are you going to go crazy?

MARIA

How do I know? What do crazy people do?

HELENA

Wait a minute. You're telling me you're afraid of going crazy. But you don't know what crazy people do. What does it mean to be crazy?

MARIA

How should I know? I'm not crazy.

HELENA

Then how will you ever know if you're crazy?

MARIA

I don't know. Maybe I won't know anybody. I won't know anything.

HELENA

If you won't know anything, you won't know you're crazy. So what's the problem?

MARIA

You ask hard questions.

(Play continues; MARIA picks up trick #5)

HELENA

Well, ya know, if you wouldn't know you're crazy . . . maybe you're *already* crazy.

MARIA

So then I should go and live with the crazy people.

HELENA

You already are.

MARIA

Don't say that. Who?

HELENA

Me.

MARIA

I thought you were okay.

HELENA

But what if I say I'm crazy?

MARIA

Then your poor husband is living with two crazy women.

HELENA

Oh . . . and *he's* not crazy?

MARIA

NO! No, he's not.

HELENA

I ask him, "Are you hungry?" He says, "No, I'm not hungry. I ate the other day." Then he goes right to the cupboard, opens it, grabs a stack of Ritz crackers and eats them while he's standing up and staring into the shelves. Not crazy?

MARIA

(Chuckles as she starts to pick up trick #6; notices that something is wrong)
Why are there five cards in this trick?

HELENA

I don't know. Somebody must have played twice. . . . Wait a minute. We should each have five cards. . . . You only have four. Here, take one back.

(MARIA picks up winning trick #6 and starts the next trick)

MARIA

What shall I say to the psychiatrist when I go?

HELENA

Whatever you want.

MARIA

(THEY complete trick #7, which MARIA wins)
I have to tell him that all the pills I'm taking aren't helping that much. The *really* bad fears. They keep coming.

HELENA

What bad fears?

MARIA

I'm afraid I'm going to get sick. I'm afraid I'm going crazy. I might do something terrible. Sometimes it gets very bad. I don't know if I can take it.

HELENA

So what's the worst thing? Are you going to kill yourself? Are you going to kill someone else?

MARIA

Ooh, NO, no. I'm good. No, no, I would never want to hurt anyone. But I'm afraid to look at knives. And what about poison?

HELENA

Well, you could think about it this way . . . even if you wanted to kill yourself or someone else, you couldn't. Where are you going to buy the poison? You can't drive anymore. You can't shop anymore. You can't even walk. Your arms and shoulders hurt. You move like a twisted turtle. . . . Even if you got hold of a knife, you're not strong enough to do anything with it. You can't even cut *soft* bread.

MARIA

Why do you talk like this? Why do you say that word, *kill?* You say bad things I don't even let myself think about. Now I'm going to think about them more! It's not good to think those thoughts.

HELENA

So what? They're just thoughts!

MARIA

I'm afraid. If *I* have those thoughts . . . I might . . . scream.

HELENA

So . . . scream.

MARIA

No! What would anybody think?

HELENA

(Lets out an extended, piercing scream as she jumps out of her chair, throws her arms up in the air, runs around the room, shouting)

I can't stand it anymore! I can't stand it! I HATE IT!

MARIA

(Startled and then horrified)

Oh, no. Oh. No! STOP! That's horrible! Your face doesn't look like you. What an awful face! Now you're really crazy!

HELENA

(Stops screaming, takes a deep breath, and calmly sits down again)

How do I look now? Can you see my face? Do I look crazy?

MARIA

(Studying her daughter)

No.

HELENA

So first I screamed . . . and now I'm okay.

MARIA

Is it really okay to do that? Are you just making this up for me? What do other people think about this? Do you do this in front of your husband? What does he think? It's too weird. I couldn't ever do that!

HELENA

Why not?

MARIA

(THEY play trick #8, which MARIA wins)

(MARIA pauses. Looks up. Pushes down on the wheelchair arms to raise herself. After a couple of tries, she's standing—as best she can. Then she musters up the courage to get out a scream—as best she can)

I *hate* it!

(In spite of her relatively weak scream, MARIA startles herself and finally falls back into the wheelchair)

(MARIA composes herself and she leads the next card)

HELENA

What was that?

MARIA

I screamed.

HELENA

How did it feel?

MARIA

Kinda crazy.

What did you just put down? You're supposed to follow suit.

HELENA

Oh, yeah. Right.

(Changes card)

MARIA

(MARIA wins trick #9)

Instead of always talking about crazy, why don't we talk about *sensible* sometimes?

HELENA

Okay, so let's do that.

MARIA

(THEY play the next trick and MARIA wins trick #10)

(MARIA starts to giggle)

HELENA

What are you giggling about?

MARIA

I don't know. When you said we could talk about sensible, I couldn't find anything to say!

HELENA

(Starts to laugh)

MARIA

(MARIA joins HELENA in contagious laughter without knowing why)

What are *you* laughing about?

HELENA

I'm thinking. What's sensible?

(Speaking in monotonous cadence)

This is the table. Here is a chair. The flowers are in the garden and the trees are in the woods. Not very interesting. . . . Maybe all the *fun* is in the crazy.

MARIA

(Enjoying herself)

Yeah, I haven't gone crazy yet after sixty-five years of worrying about it. Who am I kidding? What do I want? I'm ninety-one years old!

(Starts the last trick)

Just because I haven't gone crazy yet, doesn't mean I won't.

HELENA

(Playing cards)

I know.

MARIA

Now what am I going to tell the psychiatrist when we go to him?

HELENA

Whatever you want.

MARIA

(MARIA wins trick #11)

(Counting her tricks)

Look. I've already got ten tricks. You've got one. What was the bid?

HELENA

Three clubs.

MARIA

I think I'm winning!

HELENA

I think so too, Mom.

LIGHTS OUT

Worry to Wisdom

F or the five years my mother lived with Bob and me, I kept almost feverishly recording stories she would tell, conversations we would have, utterances she made that I never thought I'd hear from my mother. I wanted to hold on to them, humorous and heartfelt, knowing the day would come that I would no longer have her to hold on to.

❧ *Chicken Pot Pie* ❧

We were sitting at our kitchen table having chicken pot pie for lunch one day when my mother bemoaned, "I think my life would be easier if I were more religious, if I went to church."

"You do go to church," I answered.

"What are you talking about?"

"Mom, you worship at the temple of fear. It's called the Worry Church. Every day you go up to the altar and you pray. 'Dear God, forgive me my sins. Today for ten minutes I forgot to worry.'"

Channeling my father's "funniness" to ease her propensity for worry worked. She actually giggled that time and then changed the subject. "This frozen chicken pot pie is better than I thought it would be. We should learn to make chicken pot pie. I always liked chicken pot pie."

"Yah, that's a good idea, Ma. I like chicken pot pie, too."

"Does your family like it?"

"No, not particularly."

"Well, don't make it then."

Wait a minute. What? She likes chicken pot pie. I like chicken pot pie, but we can't make chicken pot pie for ourselves? Bottom line, what women/mothers want doesn't count.

When she came into adulthood during the 1920s and '30s, "What do I want?" was not even up for consideration, at least not for women in her Italian community. Women should remain open and malleable, ready to conform to what the men and the children in their lives might want. In the 1950s and '60s when I came into adulthood, thanks to Betty Friedan's *The Feminine Mystique* and women's consciousness-raising, "What do I want?" became a valid consideration. Maybe we could both learn something new.

"What do you want for lunch, honey?" my mother asked one day.

"No, Mom," I asserted. "Don't ask me what I want. It's not always about me. The question is what do *you* want for lunch? This is about you learning to say what *you* want."

"Okay, but what do you want for lunch today?"

"No, it's what do *you* want for lunch today?"

"I don't know, whatever you want."

"Okay, what do you want me to want? Or else what do you want me to want you to want?"

I don't know what we had for lunch, but we did laugh.

❧ *Remember to Forget* ❧

We were in the kitchen, again, as usual. She sighed deeply. "Life is full of heartaches. Lots of hardship in this damned world. Oh, I'm sorry I said damned. It's a good world." Wistfully, she continued, "It seems that in these last ten years I'm forgetting all the bad stuff. I want to think of everything beautiful that I had. I started forgetting when I was about eighty years old. I felt good then because I never thought I'd even reach eighty. Now I'm in my nineties. I have more aches and pains. My back is killing me. I can't walk anymore. I'm in a wheelchair! But that's okay. I say, 'I'm living!' So I actually feel better now than when I was eighty.

"That's the way to live a long life," she pronounced. "That's the way to be happy. Forget the bad stuff. *Hmmm*—I don't know if that's true, but I feel better when I think that way.

"Funny," she added, "I never thought about it before, but happiness is the same as sadness. They both make the blood rush to my head. But I do like the happiness blood rush better."

She paused for a while and added, "What's this conversation? When I was young I would've remembered. . . . Now I forgot."

I waited for her to bring up one of her many long-standing fears . . . Alzheimer's.

To my amazement she said, "It's okay. So what! It's good to forget, because then you can remember all over again." We both smiled.

❧ *Good and Evil* ❧

"I've had a terrible dream," she said one day. "A dream of opposite things. It was the opposite of what I believe. I always believed you had to be good and faithful. Any woman who looked at a man or let him look at her was a whore. I was a good kid. And I never went to bars where people might see me and think I was *that* kind of woman." She paused and added thoughtfully, "But, of course, if I had gone to one of those places, I would be seeing them and I would know what kind of people they are. Then we'd both know we were *those* kind of people. But in the dream, to be decent was wrong. It was a scary dream."

Playing solitaire a while later, she said, "I had a beautiful conversation in my brain. I wasn't going to tell you or anybody. Not everybody has to know that I talked in my brain for about two hours about good and bad, a conversation I never had before. I never thought I was good. But then I thought, I can't say that I'm that bad. But then I thought, I can't be that good either. I had a lot of friends—some liked me and some didn't like me. So little by little I finally thought I had a little of each—good and bad."

"That's great, Mom," I said. "What a great conversation you had about the good and bad in all of us."

"You say great," she answered. "But maybe it's stupid. Now that I'm old, and have nothing to do, my brain just keeps thinking stupid things. My mother would've said, 'If you had some housework and cooking to do, you wouldn't be having stupid conversations in your brain.'"

"So what is it, Mom? A beautiful or a stupid conversation?"

"Beautiful," she said, "I feel better when I think that way."

❧ *Five Beautiful Years* ❧

The days dwindled down to a precious few. Mom began to look really tired. She didn't have much of an appetite. I panicked inside. *She could die. Ninety years old. Not a bad age to get to. I don't want her to die. But maybe her time is coming. How do I deal? How do I accept?*

One morning when I walked into the kitchen for breakfast, I could see she had already had her morning coffee and a bit of toast. I went to check in on her. She was still asleep. So I went about my business—a little breakfast, phone calls, some paper work, wondering how I would ever catch up with all I had to do. Before I knew it, I felt hungry for lunch and thought Mom might be, too. She was still asleep—and very still. I watched her carefully. I wondered: *Are the covers over her moving? Where is the slight rising and falling of the covers that would assure me she is still breathing? Sometimes I can't tell if the breath I'm sensing in her is hers or mine.*

I waited and waited until I knew—for sure. Yes, I was breathing and so was she. Forty years ago I peered in on my children this way. And now I peered in on her as she once peered in on me. Our breaths encircled each other.

She was ninety-one years old now, and needing full-time care. The visiting nurse who came to evaluate her said the words that were not true for me as she spoke them, but I heard them, and they made all the difference, "You're a good daughter. It's just time."

"I'm glad the nurse agrees with me," my mother said. "For so long I kept saying, 'Helena, I'd like to go in the nursing home. It bothers me to see you doing so much. You're getting older now, too.' At first you would say, 'Don't talk like that.

It's *not* too much.' I began to have hope when you changed from 'Don't talk like that' to 'We'll see.' Still it took another two and a half years of 'We'll see' until you finally agreed I could go. Of course, there's no place like home, and I know it'll be hard for both of us. But it's time. You'll come see me there. We'll talk on the phone. We can't be together forever. We've had five beautiful years."

❧ The Next Adventure ❧

At ninety-one, my mother went off to her "next adventure" at St Patricks Manor Nursing Home, content that I wouldn't "have to worry about her so much." I continued to keep a notebook handy to capture her words, playful and poignant, which for me chronicled her journey from worry to wisdom.

In the nine years before she died, as her abilities and faculties slowly waned, we were gifted with yet another lifetime together.

❧ The Telephone Call ❧

One day, as I walked into her room at St Patricks, she cried out, "Where were you? I was just calling you on my phone, and you didn't answer!"

"Let me see the number you were dialing. That's the wrong number, Mom."

"I've been trying to call so many times."

"But you've been dialing the wrong number. Here's the right number. Now remember, I have a message machine."

"I never had a message machine."

"I know, Mom, that's why we'll practice. Now dial the right number."

She dialed, waited three seconds, looked up at me and exclaimed, "There's no answer!"

"That's okay, Mom. Let it ring a little longer. You'll hear my voice on the message machine."

"There's a voice?" she asked.

"Yes, Mom, it'll be my voice. So when you call, leave me a message. That's how I'll know to call you back."

"There's no answer," she blurted out.

"Wait . . . for the voice . . . to come on."

"Somebody's talking!" she exclaimed.

"Yeah, that's my voice, Mom."

"Hello, hello, Helena," she shouted. "You're not there."

"I know, Mom, I'm here."

"Good. Now we can go eat."

❧ *Death Is* ❧

"Honey," she said, "I realized a couple days ago I wasn't young anymore. I feel like an old lady. I feel like life is over. That I'll be leaving soon. I know you'll be sad, but I don't want you to cry too much. I've had a beautiful life, even with all my worries. And I'm not afraid of dying the way I used to be. Well sometimes, but not like before. I know it's going to happen when I'm not afraid. I'm thinking that when I fall asleep, I'll just go. Without the anxieties or the fears, I'll just leave in my sleep."

"That's how Daddy went, remember, Mom?"

"Oh, yeah, he didn't have any pain. He just slept."

"Oh, Mom! I hope I can get to be like you."

"Honey," she said as her eyes closed, "you just have to keep telling yourself over and over, 'Don't be scared. Don't be scared.' Everybody else did it. You can to do it, too. We all have to go and soon it's my turn. Maybe two or three weeks, maybe a month or two, or maybe a year. I'm just a little sorry I have to die. I would like to have a little longer to remember all the old stories." She paused. "I never knew I would accept death so well. It's really a surprise to me." She smiled and then began to giggle.

"What is it, Mom?"

"Someone on the other side of my ear just said to me, 'What are you going to do? Complain-a City Hall?'"

"Who did it sound like, Mom?"

She laughed heartily. "Your father! He always made me laugh. What's my husband's name?" Still laughing, "Oh yeah, Nick! When you're young, you cry. When you get old, you laugh. Too bad he died. He would have had so much fun making jokes about getting older. When he was seventy, he'd tell people he was ninety-five, just to make them laugh."

❧ It's the Last Bid ❧

The day came when we played our last special mother-daughter bridge game. She was ninety-two. She had forgotten how to bid, how to count tricks, how to remember what trumps were, where the lead was. It was sad. I was sad.

"Today," she said, "I thought I might [and she spelled out the dreaded word] D-I-E. But then I thought if I died, I wouldn't even know *how* I died. . . . Oh, I'm so tired. I have so many pains. I don't know why God's making me live so long.

Maybe she loves me, and she wants me to stay here, or maybe she hates me and she wants me to stay here."

She saw me scribbling.

"Helena, don't write that down. I'll just keep these stupid thoughts in my head. But maybe that's worse. Okay. Write it down. But you write whatever you want to, because I can't think."

❧ *Forget to Remember* ❧

When I returned home late one evening after a storytelling event, there was a message on my answering machine from a nurse at St Patricks. "We can't settle your mother down. We've never seen her like this. She's off the wall, crying out for her husband, screaming over and over again, 'What have you done with him? We came here together last week. He went to play cards and he hasn't come back. Don't you know he has young children?' It's so unlike her. Could you please come talk to her to calm her down? We keep trying to tell her that he died, but she won't be convinced. She says we're lying to her and just trying to calm her down."

I immediately called St Patricks. "She's asleep now," the nurse said. "She finally exhausted herself. She was severely dehydrated and had been vomiting. We blew three veins trying to get an IV in to hydrate her tonight. No need for you to come now. It would only disturb her. She needs the rest after what she's been through." *Things change. Things go downhill.*

My mother rallied slowly over the next few days, as her fluid intake increased. But it's a funny kind of rallying that never goes back to a previous level of functioning. You land on a new plateau, where you hope you can rest for a while.

One morning when she had regained some of her strength, I walked into her room and found her lying peacefully with her untouched breakfast still sitting on the tray. Calmly she told me, "They're keeping Daddy from me."

"No, Mommy, Daddy died eight years ago, and that's when you came to live with me."

"No." She shook her head, questioning me now. "We came together last week. He went to play cards and never came back."

She continued, "I know you won't lie to me, but I don't remember living at your house. I don't remember Daddy dying. Was there a funeral? Was he in a coffin? Oh, I don't know why my mind is doing these funny things. I believe what you're saying, but it's not real to me. I was never a widow."

"Maybe you've never felt like a widow, Mom."

"That's right. I think I hear him all the time. He's always right there next to me."

"Mom, when I come back later today, do you want me to bring some stuff from Mercadante's to show you he did have a funeral? And there are so many wonderful condolence cards I can bring."

"Yes," she said, "bring them all."

When I returned that afternoon, I asked, "Mom do you remember I was here this morning?"

"No. I don't remember."

A moment later she asked, "Did you bring the stuff from Mercadante's?"

❧ How Old Are We? ❧

"I don't know why I feel so bad, today," my mother said.

"You're ninety-five years old," I said.

"Are you a hundred and five, then?"

"No, I'm your daughter. I'm twenty-seven years younger than you."

"Wow. I didn't know I was ninety-five. I *feel* seventy-five. How old are you?" she asked.

"I'm sixty-eight. I *feel* ninety-five."

"Let's forget the clock," she said. "Let the clock say what it wants to say. Whatever you say you are, that's what you are. Now, I feel fifty-five, not ninety-five, maybe even thirty five. Whatever your age, it's the age you *feel*. That's what counts. Well . . . it's *food* that counts . . . if you like to eat good food."

We both smiled. It was a moment out of space and time. I realized how devastating it would be to lose her. At whatever age, there will never have been enough time. There will always have been more to say, another story to hear.

❧ *To Tell or Not to Tell* ❧

"I have a secret I wasn't going to tell you, Helena. Maybe they are trying to get rid of me. They'll be happier if I go. I might be happier if I go. Whenever I think of it, I say it's okay, but then when I think it's close, I get scared. One minute I'm scared, the next it's okay. I woke up in the night crying and crying, thinking how sad it is. I don't know what to do? Should I go or not? . . . Oh, I hope you're not crying, honey."

"Yes, I am crying, Mom, but it's not a suffering crying, it's a beautiful sadness."

"Oh, that's it," she said. "I didn't think of it that way. It is sad. And it's beautiful. All the problems you have in the family, when you're old all that's left is how much you love your family. I didn't know if I should tell you or not. But now I feel better."

"I'm glad you told me. It makes everything real. That's what it's all about. . . . I love you, Mom."

"I love you, too, honey, so much, so very much, everything. Now when I go, don't feel I'm gone forever. Every time you think about me I want you to think about the Love and the Happiness. Even thinking about the Love and the Happiness is living."

❧ *Mornings are Better than Afternoons* ❧

One afternoon when I visited her she said, "I wish I could fly home. There's no family in this place. Is Mama okay? My mother's gone? And why did you keep it from me? What must everyone have thought? The oldest daughter and she wasn't there when her mother and father died." My mother began to sob. "Oh, how horrible. Will you take me home? Tomorrow? If not tomorrow, when?"

This was not like her. It broke my heart. But it was afternoon, a more difficult time of day for those with dementia. It's called Sundowner's Syndrome.

I wondered how she would be when I visited the next morning. She was calm and clear. Mornings are always better than afternoons.

"Honey, I just woke up. I want you to be brave. About life. You live and then you die, and then you live and then you die again, over and over—that's the life."

My tears flowed freely.

"No, honey. Please, don't cry, don't be sad. Please, I love you so much. I don't think anybody had the love like us.

That's something to live for. Please don't cry. That's the world. We can't make it different. Please, please, let me feel that you're fine. I know it's hard to think about, but we can't live forever."

"I'm okay Mom, really," I said, bittersweet tears flowing, "It's just my turn for beautiful sadness."

"Yes," she said, "now it's up to the children to have a life like we had. It's great to see our children happy. And I'm so proud of my grandchildren. I'm so happy I don't want to just say it, I want you to write it down: *I have a beautiful, loving family. All my grandchildren are so special and precious. Never gave us any problems. They always gave us happiness and fun. We have a lovable family. Not to the extreme and not very low. Just normal loving for a family.*"

"Oh, oh," she started to laugh. "I'm raining again. I'm forever raining in bed. I remember the first time the nurse said I could just let it go. 'Is it okay?' I asked her. 'Is it really okay? In the bed?' And now that's all I do," she said still laughing.

"How did you get to be happy, Mom?"

"I don't know. I never hated my mother. I always loved her, but she was always cross. She never looked happy. That made me change. I didn't want to be like her. How I got to be happy? . . . " she giggled, ". . . by watching my mother not be happy."

Shifting focus, she added, "See that lady out in the hallway? I was looking at her and I asked myself, 'Why . . . ' Oh, God, I forgot what I was going to say."

"You'll remember it later," I said.

"Nah, it's gone. My body knows I've had enough and I don't have to say anymore. Isn't this a good discussion, Helena? I love it. I love it."

"I love it, too, Mom."

"Yes, a fine, a very fine discussion. I'll never forget it. . . . Oh, oh, I need to do it again. It's going to wet everything," she chuckled. "*Madonn*, it's coming. And now it's running on my red skirt and my matching blouse. Okay, it's stopping. That's all the nurse had to say to me, 'You can let it go,' and now they have to change me every time. . . . Okay, honey," she said, "we can stop this for now."

"Okay, Mom, we'll talk again. You rest and I'll go do my work. . . . Love you, Mommy."

"Love you, honey."

"Bye, Mom."

"Bye, honey."

❧ Twisting into Another Direction ❧

We were having tea and cookies one day in the St Patricks cafe. She gazed out the window, her eyes growing distant. She wiped a few crumbs off the table. Then she said, "I feel like I've twisted into another direction. I'm fading away."

And then she just seemed to float off somewhere, where I couldn't reach her. I began to weep silently. Gone was the mother I knew.

She'd always been the kind of mother who watched you like a hawk. From across any room we were in, she would notice every slight shift of expression on my face, always ready for some disaster: "What is it, honey? What's the matter? Are you okay?" I remember how annoyed I'd get whenever she did that.

And now here we were, our faces but two feet apart, and she never noticed the tears streaming down my cheeks.

❧ *Five Last Years* ☙

My mother slipped slowly away the last final years . . . from age ninety-five to her death three weeks before her 100th birthday. Like life at any age, there were ups and downs, setbacks and rallies.

During one setback, we thought she was really gone. She'd stopped eating and drinking. She was sleeping all the time. The nurses and aides hugged and comforted me. It seemed the end had come, so they took away all her pills, whereupon she rallied and looked forward to not another week, or month, but what became at least two more years. Another medical crisis, another rebound.

❧ *She's Lethargic* ☙

It was one of the down times that were happening more often. "She's lethargic these days," the nurses told me. When I visited her then, she was often sitting in her wheelchair, slumped over, eyes closed. I remembered when such a sight would have been too horrifying for me to look at. Slowly over some forty years, I'd been able to not only look at it, but be with it. Still it hurt. There was a heaviness in my heart each time I walked into the nursing home. I was fearful of what I might see.

When I walked away from the nursing home, the heaviness in my heart was the ever-growing knowing that no number of rallies would reverse the inevitable. My mother would die.

She was often in a state of reverie, neither here nor there. What could bring her peace, calm, and happiness was having a baby (doll, though it was) to hold all day long, to cover up, to cuddle, to kiss, to protect. The nurses sometimes said that when she was restless, in her dream-like state, she'd try to move around, get up, tidy things up, or at least she'd imagine tidying things up. Somewhere she was still taking care of us, cooking, cleaning.

ᴥ *Five Kisses* ᴤ

It was extra hard this time. We went to the St Patricks dining room for a special performance—a man at the mic, I can't remember what he was playing—an accordion? He stood and sang, and some of it was loud enough for her to hear.

We sat close. We held hands. I leaned over into her, our heads touching.

We kissed in that way she kissed children and grandchildren—five times at a clip. *Mmwha, mmwha, mmwha, mmwha, mmwha.*

She may not have known me, but she KNEW me.

Only then it seemed she remembered my father, her husband, Nick, for the first time in a long time.

"Where is he? Why isn't he here?" she asked.

"It's okay, Mom. He's not here, but he IS here."

"He's alright?"

"Yes," I said.

"They're taking care of him?"

"Yes."

"As long as he's not locked up."

"He's safe, Mom."

We held and touched, and she knew that I knew that she knew. Loving energy flowed between us. I let it in. I don't always. It's too hard sometimes, until I remember beautiful sadness. When they wheeled her back to her room, she didn't wave happily good-bye as she usually did. She pointed at me as the elevator door closed, "No, I want to go home with HER."

❧ *Winter* ☙

It was winter and holiday time. My ninety-seven-year-old mother was having a bad day when I visited. She'd had so many good days lately . . . pleasant, engaged.

But this was one of her days of being lost and fearful. She was desperate for her mother.

"Mama, where are you? Where are you? Where is she? Where is she? Mama, Mama! What are we going to do!"

"It's okay," I said. "She's okay. It's all okay. *Shhhh*."

"I think they're going to kill us. . . ."

"No, no, Mom," I tried to soothe her. And I imagined my ninety-seven-year-old mother as a desperate young child, crying for the lost mother, in fear for her family's safety. When it came time for me to go back home—she said, "I know if you go, I'll die."

Who is mother? Who is daughter?

Then she said, "I feel my mother and father and sisters and brother around me."

Is there anything to the idea of crossing over and being greeted by loved ones? I don't know. But a chill ran up my spine.

"Go now," the aide said to me, "You've got your life to live, too. She's asleep. We'll take care of her."

These caretakers—they are angels amongst us. They walk quietly and unseen.

Not until afterward did I realize that day was probably
December 2, the day my Dad died eleven years before. This is
a tough time of year. So dark, so cold, so still, so done. But
soon the light will begin to peek through . . . and grow . . . and
grow.

❧ *A Poem* ❧

It's dark in the middle of the night
A tear finds its way down onto my pillow

My mother says she'll be going soon
My father left already

When the light dawns, deadness clings to the bones and
    sinews of her body
Is today the day?
Then more slowly than the sun rises, the quivering breath of
    life insists its way into being
The current that enlivens will flow one more day

My mother says she'll be going soon
My father left already

What is that moment before the last?
In that pregnant unknown space
In that exit push of life, what do we birth?
Can you see?
Can you see the crowning?

◆ *Words to Remember* ◆

The markers of decline continued . . . a little less eating, a little less drinking, a little less speaking, a little less being awake. The time came when it was harder and harder to understand what she was staying. She'd struggle to get out a word, and then it might be unintelligible. Scrambled words. Shredded meaning.

Where are you Mom? When was our last real conversation? What is happening in your dream of now which differs from your yesterday's dream? I can still feel you, Mom, but it's a jumble.

And yet there were moments near her end days when the gems flowed clearly from my mother's lips:

"I have a stupid thought. I love everybody in the world. I must have a very strong heart. Still . . . it's hard to love everybody . . . all the time. Separate, sometimes, but not for too long."

◆◆

"If we want a joy, we create one. I don't know where I'm going in this wheelchair, or what I'm doing, but wherever I go, whatever I do, I know I'll love it. We meet, we live, it's wonderful. That's why I feel happy all the time. How can people live angry all the time?"

◆◆

"It's not *live* and *die*. It's *live* and *love*. The *loving* never disappears." Tears were streaming down my face. But this time, unlike five years earlier, she noticed. She looked at them and said, "That's the joy dripping out of you because of love."

≈ જ

My mother? My guru? All the time I've searched for wisdom *out there*, I never imagined that it was always right *beside me*—just waiting—to break free.

≈ Ten Years Later જ

Ten years after my mother died, I heard Richard Moss, a leader in consciousness transformation, recount a story about the Dalai Lama: "When the Dalai Lama was asked why he still spoke so respectfully of the Chinese, even though they had invaded Tibet and done atrocious things to the Tibetan people, he said, 'I speak that way because I feel better.'"

Is that you again, Mom? Those are your words almost exactly! "That's the way to be happy. Forget the bad stuff. *Hmmm*—I don't know if that's true, but I feel better when I think that way."

I see you now, Mom. I can hear you and I'm smiling. By the way, there are a bunch of things I forgot to ask you. What did you and Daddy talk about the night you were married? And what was your mother's mother's maiden name?

Afterword

Thank you to my readers who journeyed with me through my stories, and who appreciate that though our individual stories differ, what connects us is the one Human Journey we all share. When we tell and listen to each other's unique stories, our vistas expand. We see we're not alone. We learn from and understand each other better. Empathy and compassion grow.

Where am I personally on that journey we all share? First of all, I've given up trying to get anywhere. I have no idea where I'm going to end up on this journey . . . well, wait a minute . . . I'm eighty-four years old now and I *do* know, ultimately, where I'm going to end up.

Secondly, I take to heart the wisdom of another guru, Yogi Berra. "When you get to a fork in the road, take it." So I continue to follow the impulse to live out loud and put one foot in front of the other, wherever it leads.

I keep reminding myself (and this is hard work!) that there is *no where* to get. It's never the destination. It's the journey itself . . . the people you meet along the way . . . the love, laughter, and joy you create with another, with many others, and fingers crossed, one day, hopefully, with everyone—story, by story, by story.

I remain . . .

Still living.
Still laughing.
Still loving.
Still loud.

Acknowledgments

Thank you to my children, my husband, my extended family, and dear friends who supported and encouraged me to bring my storytelling impulses onto the stage. Special thank you to my daughter, Maria. Without her editing, patience, and love, these stories would never have made it to the page.

About the Author

Helena Leet Pellegrini, Ph.D., is a psychologist, mentor, cancer survivor, and award-winning storyteller. She has performed at storytelling venues across the country, including the storied Club Passim and Story Space in Cambridge, Boulder Fringe Festival in Colorado, and MassMouth Storytelling Grand Slam in Boston.

Helena is a mother of three and grandmother of five. She lives at Southgate at Shrewsbury in Massachusetts with her dear husband of sixty-three years.

She is available on the following social media sites:
- Facebook (@helenaleetpellegrini): www.facebook.com/helena.leetpellegrini
- Goodreads (Helena Leet-Pellegrini): www.goodreads.com/user/show/113601385-helena-leet-pellegrini.

Bonus videos of select live performances can be viewed on the Fringe Tree Press website: www.fringetreepress.com.

Made in the USA
Middletown, DE
27 August 2021

47043910R00080